HABITS OF SUCCESS

THE PRINCIPLES OF DEBBIE & GOLIATH

CREATED BY MULTI #1 INTERNATIONAL BEST-SELLING AUTHOR & AWARD WINNING SPEAKER ON HABITS

ERIK SWANSON

HABITS OF SUCCESS

Copyright © 2024
THE PRINCIPLES OF DEBBIE & GOLIATH

All rights reserved. No part of this publication may be reproduced, distributed, or transmitted in any form or by any means, including photocopying, recording, or other electronic or mechanical methods, without the prior written permission of the publishers and Habitude Warrior Int., except in the case of brief quotations embodied in critical reviews and certain other noncommercial uses permitted by copyright law. For permission requests, write to the publishers, addressed "Attention: Permissions Coordinators," at *info@integritypub.com*.

Permission was granted and approved to use Celebrity Author's testimonials and contributing chapters, quotes and thoughts throughout the book series, but it is understood that each contributing author and celebrity author are their own entities and Habitude Warrior International is not responsible or endorse any opinions or actions thereby taken by said authors. Quantity sales special discounts are available on quantity purchases by corporations, associations, and others. For details, contact the publisher at the address above.

Orders by U.S. trade bookstores and wholesalers.
Email: *Team@IntegrityPub.com*

Manufactured and printed in the United States of America and distributed globally by Integrity Pub.

Library of Congress Control Number:
Hardback ISBN: 978-1-964330-05-1
Paperback ISBN: 978-1-964330-04-4

THE PRINCIPLES OF DEBBIE & GOLIATH

Legal Disclaimer & Acknowledgment

The contents of *The Principles of Debbie And Goliath* book series includes various stories, reflections, and experiences by each of our co-authors. It is important to clarify that the views, stories, principles, and opinions expressed by the individual authors in this series are solely their own and do not necessarily reflect the beliefs, policies, or positions of Habitude Warrior International LLC, Integrity Publishing, or their affiliates and partners, or the other individual authors and writers in this series.

Each chapter is the original work of its respective author. While Habitude Warrior International LLC and Integrity Publishing own the copyright rights to the content within this book series, the statements, claims, and backgrounds presented by each contributing author are their sole responsibility. These authors assert that their contributions are their original work and words, and they are accountable for the truthfulness and accuracy of their content.

The diverse collection of stories, examples, and ideas presented in this series aims to offer insights and guidance for overcoming challenges. However, readers are reminded that these narratives are based on the authors' personal experiences and perspectives. As such, not every belief or approach may resonate with or be applicable to all readers. The variety of viewpoints is intended to provide a broad spectrum of experiences and reflections, fostering a rich and diverse dialogue on the subject of empowerment and personal growth.

Furthermore, Habitude Warrior International LLC and Integrity Publishing do not guarantee any specific outcomes or results from applying the principles and strategies outlined in this series. The organizations are not liable for any consequences or effects that may arise from the application of information contained in these books. Readers are encouraged to use their discretion and judgment in interpreting and applying the ideas shared by the co-authors.

~ Habitude Warrior International LLC & Integrity Publishing

CONTENTS

Dedication	Bringing Awareness To Domestic Violence	13
Introduction	The Principles of Debbie & Goliath	17
Shaune Arnold	Conquer Your Mind & Conquer The World!	23
Alicia Couri	You Have A God-Designed Purpose	33
Amy Keiderling	Love Yourself: BE-U-TIFUL GIRL!	41
Azadeh Bennett	A Journey To Freedom	47
Dr. Betty Speaks	Navigating Life's Storms With Resilience And Divine Authority	53
Charlotte DeLon	Work On Me	63
Cynthia Gallardo	Beyond Your Goliath: The Legacy Of Synergy	69
Dr. Deborah J. Anderson	Who Do You Choose To Follow?	75
Elaine R. Sugimura	What Makes Life Meaningful	81
Eileen E. Galbriath	Mentorship To Success	83
Elizabeth Anne Walker	The Power Of Reading & Personal Development	93
Fatima Hurd	Breaking Free	99
Joanna James	My Darling Self	107
Katherine Vargas	Amazing Grace	115
Katie Mares	Navigating Challenges To Unleash The Empowered Woman Within	123
Lauren Cobb	Emotional Intellegence	131
Liz Sears	Create Your Life	137
Lorna Sherland	Self-Actualization: The Layers Built On Truth	145
M. A. Fults	Giants Among Us	149

THE PRINCIPLES OF DEBBIE & GOLIATH

Maris Segal	Dear Women Of The World	155
Mel Mason	Chaos Before The Calm	165
Dr. Onika Shirley	Not Qualified	171
Rachel Corpus	Extend Love	177
Ruthe Hage	Embracing Light On The Mentorship Journey	183
Sally Wurr	Do You Know Where You Are Going To?	185
Sarah Lee, MBA	Financial Literacy Will Save The World	195
Steph Shinabery	Finding My Voice & Strength	201
Tammy Thacker	Breaking Boundaries: From Law Enforcement To Entrepreneurship	211
Tasha Smith	From Me To You	217
Tayler L. Cole	Confidently Leveling Up	223
Vikki Rood	From Junior High Blues To Etsy Hues: A Story Of Resilience	233
Female Empowerment Resources	The Principles of Debbie & Goliath	239

Global Speakers Mastermind & Habitude Warrior Masterminds

Join us and become a member of our tribe! Our Global Speakers Mastermind is a virtual group of amazing thinkers and leaders who meet twice a month. Sessions are designed to be 'to the point' and focused while sharing fantastic techniques to grow your mindset as well as your pocketbooks. We also include famous guest speaker spots for our private Masterclasses. We also designate certain sessions for our members to mastermind with each other & and counsel on the topics discussed in our previous Masterclasses. It's time for you to join a tribe who truly cares about **YOU** and your future and start surrounding yourself with the famous leaders and mentors of our time. It is time for you to up-level your life, businesses, and relationships.

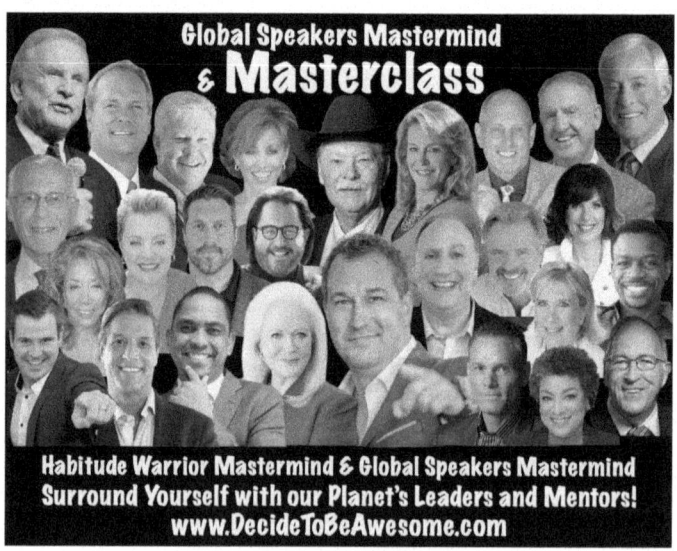

For more information to check out our Masterminds:
Team@HabitudeWarrior.com
www.DecideToBeAwesome.com

BECOME AN INTERNATIONAL
#1 BESTSELLING AUTHOR & SPEAKER

Habitude Warrior International has been highlighting award-winning Speakers and #1 Bestselling Authors for over 25 years. They know what it takes to become #1 in your field and how to get the best exposure around the world. If you have ever considered giving yourself the GIFT of becoming a well-known Speaker and a fantastically well known #1 Best-Selling Author, then you should email their team right away to find out more information in how you can become involved. They have the best of the best when it comes to resources in achieving the bestselling status in your particular field. Start surrounding yourself with the N.Y. Times Bestsellers of our time and start seeing your dreams become reality!

For more information to become a #1 Bestselling Author & Speaker on our Habitude Warrior Conferences Please text the word AUTHORS to 619-304-6268 And also go to:
www.DecideToBeAwesome.com

HABITS OF SUCCESS

DEDICATION

BRINGING AWARENESS TO DOMESTIC VIOLENCE

We strive to bring awareness to issues that are prevalent in our world today. Our goal is to assist in identifying these issues in order for us to collectively come together to help eradicate them. Our first book in *The Principles of Debbie & Goliath* series is dedicated to the awareness of Domestic Violence. Domestic violence is a pattern of abusive behavior in a relationship that is used by one partner to gain or maintain power and control over another intimate partner. It can occur between spouses, partners, or within any type of intimate relationship. Domestic violence can take various forms, including physical abuse, emotional or psychological abuse, sexual abuse, economic abuse, and stalking.

Common signs of domestic violence may include:

Physical Abuse: This involves any use of physical force with the intent to cause harm, such as hitting, slapping, punching, or kicking.

Emotional or Psychological Abuse: This includes behaviors that aim to control, manipulate, or demean the victim. Examples include verbal abuse, constant criticism, and isolation from friends and family.

Sexual Abuse: Any non-consensual sexual activity or coercion falls under sexual abuse. This can involve forced sex, demeaning comments about one's body, or any other form of sexual mistreatment.

Economic Abuse: This involves controlling the victim's financial resources, making it difficult for them to be financially independent. This can include withholding money, preventing access to resources, or sabotaging employment opportunities.

Stalking: Persistent, unwanted attention and contact, either online or offline, can be a form of domestic violence. This includes monitoring someone's activities without their consent.

It's important to note that domestic violence can affect anyone regardless of age, race, gender, socioeconomic status, or education level. It is a serious and widespread issue with significant consequences for the individuals involved and society as a whole.

If you or someone you know is experiencing domestic violence, it is crucial to seek help. There are numerous resources available, including domestic violence hotlines, shelters, counseling services, and legal support. In many countries, there are laws and services in place to protect victims of domestic violence and hold perpetrators accountable for their actions. We have listed some resources in the back of this book for you. If you are in immediate danger, contact your local emergency services.

For a list of resources, please turn to page 239.

THE PRINCIPLES OF DEBBIE & GOLIATH

HABITS OF SUCCESS

INTRODUCTION

THE PRINCIPLES OF DEBBIE & GOLIATH

In the heart of every woman lies a story of resilience, a tale of overcoming, and a triumph of success... much like the story of David and Goliath. Yet, in our modern world, the challenges faced are often more nuanced, complex, and deeply intertwined with the fabric of societal expectations and personal struggles. *The Principles of Debbie and Goliath* book series is a beacon of hope and female empowerment, designed to guide and inspire women of all ages.

This series is a unique compilation of wisdom, experiences, and strategies from various women, including celebrities and thought leaders, each sharing their insights to uplift and empower. Each volume in this series is dedicated to a specific theme, resonating with the different stages of a woman's journey towards self-awareness and empowerment.

This series is unique in that it is 100% female empowered and co-authored. Each of the three books in the series will include 33 female Co-Authors and one female Celebrity Author. Each author teaches principles on how to conquer obstacles in life and how to handle them for ultimate success to become a truly global empowered female. Each Co-Author's chapter focuses on the perspective of giving their younger female 13-year-old self advice, suggestions, and counsel to become an empowered female leader in life, and is sure to become a blueprint for the female teenager's success journey around the globe! Our goal is to empower females and empower our world in beautiful harmony.

Volume 1: Habits of Success

In our first volume, we delve into the 'Habits of Success.' This book is a treasure trove of practical advice and motivational stories, focusing on developing a strong sense of self, cultivating resilience, and fostering a mindset geared towards success. From navigating self-confidence issues to mastering financial literacy, this volume is designed to equip female readers with the habits and tools necessary to create a foundation of personal female empowerment.

Volume 2: Focus & Alignment

The second volume, 'Focus & Alignment,' shifts the lens to the importance of aligning one's values, goals, and actions. Here, we explore the art of maintaining focus amidst life's myriad challenges. This volume tackles topics such as dealing with relationship dynamics, understanding situational awareness, and overcoming societal pressures, all crucial for aligning our female reader's inner compass towards personal and professional fulfillment.

Volume 3: Global Female Empowerment

In our final volume in this series, 'Global Female Empowerment,' the narrative extends beyond individual struggles, addressing issues that impact females on a global scale. This book is an homage to the collective power of women, discussing habits and strategies to allow our young female readers to not have to reinvent the wheel, but to learn from our Co-Author's experiences. It's a call to action for women to unite in their diversity, strength, and resilience to effect positive change in the world.

The Principles of Debbie and Goliath is more than a book series; it's a female movement! It's a conversation between generations—from the Co-Authors to their 13-year-old selves. Each story in the series shares principles toward understanding and overcoming the unique challenges that women face in today's society. Join us on this empowering journey, and discover how to turn your challenges into stepping stones for success.

ERIK SWANSON

Multi #1 Best-Selling Author, International Award Winning Speaker, Creator of *The Principles of Debbie & Goliath*, Founder of Habitude Warrior International and Integrity Publishing

HABITS OF SUCCESS

> You are the only one who gets to decide what you will be remembered for.
>
> ~ Taylor Swift

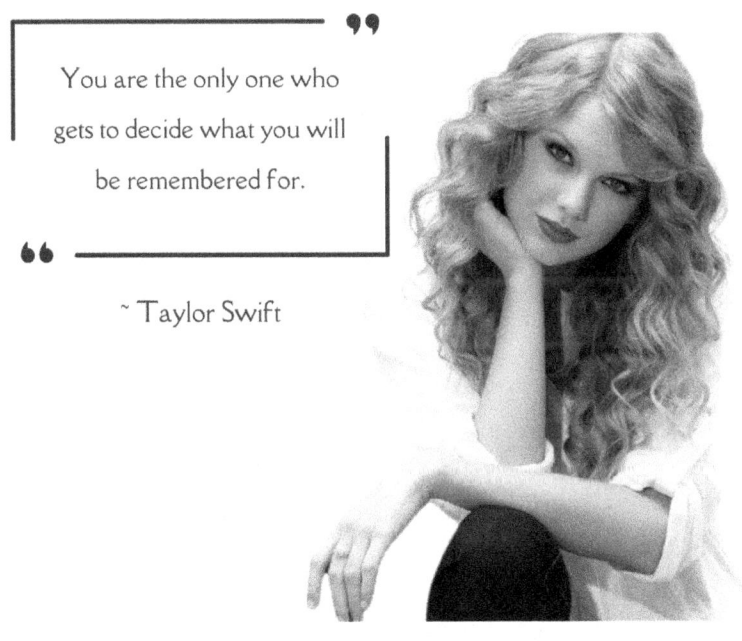

HABITS OF SUCCESS

SHAUNE ARNOLD

CONQUER YOUR MIND & CONQUER THE WORLD!

*"Starlight, star bright, the first star I see tonight.
I wish I may, I wish I might, get the wish I wish tonight!"*

My dearest Debbie, this has been your most passionate and long-lasting prayer. You want so much from this life, as well you should. You are a unique and beautiful spark of life, capable of creating absolute magnificence in everything that you touch. The world can be scary. Being a girl is tough—*but you are so much tougher, my love!*

HABITS OF SUCCESS

I know you, Debbie. As you become a young woman, you want both protection and freedom. You want people to see you without revealing yourself. You are so brave. Yet you're very, very afraid so much of the time, feeling like a jumbled mass of contradictions. It's all completely normal.

Let me give you some advice, my dear. If you see the world as evil and harsh, you will surely be its victim. Love is all there is. Everything else is an illusion. I want to help you discover how to live your life from a place of love; for yourself, for humanity and the earth. This is how you will create the life that you truly want. Why is this so? What's love got to do with it? This is so because the things you think about will always guide your decisions. Your decisions, in turn, guide your actions—*and your actions will create your life*.

Each choice you make, and everything you do daily, impacts your future. Even the simple decisions to get out of bed, go to school with your homework done, and avoid trouble along the way, create your future. *Think about it.* If you get As and Bs in middle school and high school, colleges will give you scholarships and grants to help pay for your rent, food, clothes, books, and everything you need until you're out of college. Honey, that work is done *now, today*, while you're in middle school and high school. Once you reach college age, it'll be too late to do that work.

Once you get into college, choosing a major and passing your classes with good grades will help you land a great job, or start your own business in your mid to late 20s and early 30s. I know that's a long, long time from now, but the time will pass by like a bolt of lightning! You have to be on your toes, Deb. You have to be ready for the world. You have to guard your thoughts and learn to control your mind so you can control your future.

So, where do the things you think about come from? How can you control your thoughts when the bullies come around? How can you stay strong when your siblings mock you and your parents and teachers don't support your dreams? "Frenemies" are everywhere. How can you become your very best friend and strongest supporter in the face of all this nonsense?

THE PRINCIPLES OF DEBBIE & GOLIATH

You do it by choosing love, choosing happiness, and choosing to be your very best friend. Yes, these are choices! You can choose to be angry or sad, or you can choose to be happy and live in love, no matter what is going on around you. No situation lasts forever. No one that is in your life today, and causing you problems, will be there forever. If you are being physically or emotionally harmed, *get help immediately*! Don't stay in a dangerous situation. If you are not being injured, however, you can choose to put up with people or situations that merely annoy you. Understand that it's temporary. Eventually, it will change. The semester will end. That person will move on or forget you.

When you think this way consciously, as each hard situation happens, after a while the choice to be different will sink into your unconscious mind. You will begin to naturally think, feel, and act from this place of love, peace, and happiness.

Know that this change in thinking takes work! You may be dealing with a lot of negative feelings already crowding your unconscious mind from years and years of bullies, siblings, parents, and teachers trampling your feelings and dreams. Let me help you unclog your unconscious mind and discover how to insert new thoughts and feelings in there to help you build the life that you really want to live.

Please understand that your unconscious mind is as old as you are. Before you were seven, it absorbed everything adults said to you about yourself and the world, good or bad. So, what do you remember hearing when you were very young? Did anyone tell you things like, "Don't talk to strangers" before you left the house? That served you when you were seven, but you are growing up.

Are you afraid to try out for the cheerleading squad because some *feeling* you can't even name makes you think you're clumsy or unworthy? Do you dream of performing in a school play, but you tell yourself you can't, that you're untalented and people will laugh? You just sit in the auditorium, watching others have fun instead. Did some grown up tell you that you're dumb, and that math is hard, *and now you think you can't do math*?

HABITS OF SUCCESS

Be aware, these are all thoughts that you let sink into your unconscious mind, and they are holding you back. It's not your fault. You were so young that you had no filter. You had no way of knowing they were wrong. You didn't understand that you're naturally smart, graceful, talented, and beautiful. You can excel at math, science, or any other subject you like. You can be a cheerleader or star in the play—*if you learn to control your thoughts and your unconscious mind.*

Your unconscious mind is as old as you are, but it responds like a young child from a place of feeling. It creates 95 percent of your beliefs, behavior, learning, change, and success. You must master your unconscious mind, Debbie, to master your success in life.

The unconscious mind is the place where your dreams and all of your deepest fears reside—*but it's your greatest friend!* It literally beats your heart for you and keeps you breathing in the middle of the night. It digests your food and seeks to keep you safe by reminding you, *"Don't talk to strangers!"*

The challenge is that your unconscious mind doesn't know you're not seven anymore. It doesn't understand that you need to explore the world fearlessly; that *you need to talk to strangers* to build your success. The key for you, Debbie, is to recognize when that fear comes up and stops you dead in your tracks. When this happens, ask yourself if the feeling you feel is true. I don't mean, ask yourself if it's real. You feel it—you know it's real. I'm saying: ask yourself if it's true.

How do you know if it's true? Well, is it true for everyone? There are cheerleaders, actors, and great math students all around you. It can't be true for *everyone*—so why is it true for *you*?

Honey, it's true for *you* because at some point in the past you heard what someone said to you about you, and you then decided you are not enough, that you don't have enough, or you don't know enough, or you don't have the right friends or support. That was a choice. You can make another choice.

THE PRINCIPLES OF DEBBIE & GOLIATH

My dearest Debbie, you can decide to live in love, for yourself (and for those that hurt you). You can make a vow to like and support yourself, *no matter what*, and to believe in your ability to do that thing (whatever it is) and get what you want. That's what Nike means by, *"Just Do It."*

Feel the fear and uncertainty if that is what comes up. Understand that it's just an emotion. Let the emotion wash through you—and then release it. Consciously think of a new, more powerful thought and create a new story for yourself; one that believes you can accomplish your goal.

Feel the power in that new thought. Think about how that new story will get you onto the squad, onto the stage, or at the head of the class. Really *feel* how good that success is in your body and in your mind. See yourself in that uniform, in the costume, or with your hand raised confidently ready to answer your teacher correctly.

Learn to Meditate to Control Your Body and Mind

Sometimes, positive thinking is not quite enough. We need tools that can help us make that shift inside. This is where meditation comes in. When we meditate, we sit quietly, concentrating on our breathing, and calmly watch our thoughts go by. We can ask a question of ourselves, God or the universe, and allow the response to flow to us.

We are not our thoughts. We observe our thoughts. Our goal in meditating is to connect with that observer and to disconnect from the thoughts. This creates space for change.

I will share a meditation method with you. You will love to meditate. It's really awesome! All you have to do is relax.

Get comfortable. It's better to sit in a comfortable chair, but you can lie on your bed if you prefer. Just know that lying on the bed can lead you to fall asleep. When you meditate, you want to relax, but you want to stay awake for the entire meditation.

Now that you are comfortable, uncross your arms and legs. You want all of the energy in your body to flow freely. Close your eyes. Just relax.

HABITS OF SUCCESS

Breathe in deeply through your nose. As you breathe in, slowly count mentally to four. Fill your lungs during that count of four. Once your lungs are full, hold your breath for another slow count of four. When you reach four, begin to slowly release your breath through your mouth in four slow counts. Repeat this breath sequence three times. You should now begin to feel relaxed.

Now, as you breathe in deeply once again, imagine a golden, sparkling ball of light, radiating love, peace and happiness coming down from above to wash over the top of your head. As you breathe in, allow that golden sparkling light to flow down into your head. Allow the light to fill your head with love, peace, and happiness.

As you slowly breathe in and out allow that wonderful, supportive light to wash down into your throat, and then into your chest, into your abdomen, your hips, your thighs, knees and calves, and then down into your feet. By the time you breathe into your feet, you will be filled with love, peace, and happiness. Stay here as long as you like. Pull this amazing feeling deep down inside yourself so that it takes root in your unconscious mind.

While you are here, visualize the life that you want, today and in the future. Ask questions of yourself, God, and the universe to help you set goals and make your plans to achieve them. What decisions do you need to make, what actions do you need to take to capture this dream and make it your reality?

Relax. Let it flow. While you meditate, answers will reveal themselves to you. They will pop into your head just like magic, and you'll wonder how you struggled over this challenge for so long. Meditation is one key you can always use to feel peaceful, to work through challenges and to map out your place in the world.

Meditate often (10 to 20 minutes every day if you can) and that new feeling will sink into your unconscious mind. It will replace that old icky feeling that you can't do something, that people don't like you, or that you're dumb. You will become confident from the inside out. You'll make powerful decisions that will create the life of your dreams, and the beautiful spark of life that is you will surely change the world.

HABITS OF SUCCESS

SHAUNE ARNOLD

Shaune B. Arnold, Esq., a distinguished attorney based in downtown Los Angeles, California, exemplifies a blend of legal expertise and compassionate advocacy. Specializing in the California Environmental Quality Act (CEQA), Shaune's practice spans public and private sectors, focusing on legal compliance issues. Her prowess extends to a robust renewable energy practice, real estate development, private placements, mergers and acquisitions, and forging strategic corporate alliances for her clients.

Shaune is an alumnus of UCLA with a BA in Psychology, and UC Hastings College of the Law, As Managing Partner of FINNEY ARNOLD LLP, Shaune has provided invaluable counsel to small businesses. Her nearly 30-year career is marked by her role as outside General Counsel, guiding start-ups, emerging growth, and established businesses across diverse industries. Her insight is shaped by personal challenges, having emancipated herself from an abusive household at age 14 through a rare legal process known as 'divorcing' her parents.

Shaune's academic contributions include teaching Business Law, Human Resources, and Ethics at a prestigious local university, alongside training professionals in Neurolinguistic Programming to help them transform their businesses and their personal lives. Shaune's experience as a licensed Financial Advisor, with Series 7, Series 63, Series 65, and California Insurance licenses, further broadens her expertise.

Shaune has also demonstrated academic excellence by joining MENSA, reflecting her exceptional intellectual abilities. Her commitment to personal growth is evident in her pursuits like golf, camping, and learning guitar.

Beyond her professional endeavors, Shaune's personal journey from adversity to advocacy is profound. As a Court Appointed Special Advocate (CASA), she channels her experiences into helping abused and neglected children, representing their interests in court.

Shaune co-authored "*Fight for Your Dreams: The Power of Never Giving Up*" with Les Brown, marking her as a #1 Amazon Best-Selling Author. Her academic accolades include the American Jurisprudence Award for Excellence in Trial Advocacy.

Shaune Arnold's story is one of resilience, legal acumen, and a relentless commitment to empowering others, particularly the most vulnerable in society.

www.FALawyers.com

HABITS OF SUCCESS

ALICIA COURI
YOU HAVE A GOD-DESIGNED PURPOSE

Dedicated to Khalida – You are beautiful and God has a plan for your life that the devil tried to destroy!

"I'm so stupid."

"I'm ugly."

"I hate being so different."

"Why can't I be more like everyone else?"

"No one will ever love me."

Have you ever had those thoughts cross your mind? What do you tell yourself when you do have those thoughts? Do you agree and accept them to be true?

Or do you fight against them?

When I was about your age, those thoughts crowded my mind. From my earliest memory, those negative, painful thoughts first came when I looked at my classmates and recognized I was so very different. Different to me was bad. I wanted to fit in and look like the other girls, but I didn't. Piled on top of my own negative thoughts, the adults around me said many of the same things.

HABITS OF SUCCESS

"You're lazy."

"Alicia, you're stupid."

"You're a dunce."

"You can't learn."

"You never finish anything."

"You're a quitter."

If that wasn't bad enough, other kids, my peers, would join in with the insults.

"Shorty pants, shorty pants."

"Ew, why is your skin so dark? It looks like poo."

"Your hair is wild and fizzy."

"You talk funny."

They would laugh at me and call me stupid when I couldn't answer the teacher's questions. I was terrified to get called on in class or to have to go up to the board to work out a math problem.

Teachers would constantly demand of me, "Why can't you be more like your sister"?

My sister was smart and beautiful and disciplined and, clearly, I was not. I wanted to yell back to them, "Because I'm not my sister." But that would be rude and disrespectful, and would have landed me in more severe punishment, so I kept my mouth shut and buried my shame and pain.

That voice, the one that began telling me all those negative things from as early as five years old, was the voice of the enemy.

The Devil never wants us to succeed, so as early in our lives as he can, he will try to tear us down with negative thoughts. He'll lead us into creating negative comparisons against others so we're always coming up short. Then, he'll enroll other people to pile it on so we can't help but believe all his lies are truths.

His greatest tool is to try to destroy the plan and purpose God has in store for us. He does it so cunningly and we fall for it, especially if we don't have the right people around us and the right teaching to overcome it.

We can so easily become overwhelmed by those negative messages that it will cause us to spiral into darkness, depression, negative destructive emotions, and suicidal thoughts.

But that is not what God intends for us. He loves us so, so very much that no matter what has happened to us, God loves us unconditionally and has a plan for our success. All it takes is for us to have a little bit of hope in that truth.

You were born in this very age for a purpose. You may not know what that is yet or even feel like you have one, but I am telling you that you were uniquely and wonderfully made by God for a reason; it's your responsibility to spend your time figuring that out.

Those lying voices that work so hard to convince you that you're broken, ugly, stupid, not enough, are meant to distract you and take you off course from that purpose. You have a unique ability that is meant to create an impact.

How do I know this?

Because, when I was your age, I really didn't believe I had anything of worth or value to share with anyone.

I didn't think I had any gifts or talents.

I wasn't smart enough to be successful, or tall or strong, or even pretty. There wasn't anything special about me.

I remember hearing my father say many times, "God didn't create us all equal—look at Michael Jackson and Michael Jordan. He definitely didn't create them like the rest of us."

I believed him; he was my dad, so why wouldn't I?

Hearing that was a big reason why I grew up believing that some people were better than the rest of us, because they had amazing talent, and we didn't. So, I looked up to those celebrities and put them on a pedestal, one so far up that kept me so low down. Do you find yourself doing that, looking at celebrities or social media influencers and thinking they are so great and you're not?

Are you totally bought into the belief like I was, that "someone like me" couldn't make a difference because I wasn't gifted like "them?"

But that was a big fat lie for me and it is for you today!

I wasted so much of my life believing that lie even though I had big dreams inside of me.

I pushed my dreams way down and was ashamed and embarrassed to admit them. Instead, I continued to believe I was a nobody that would do nothing. After all, no one expected I would amount to anything, no one thought I was anything special.

Until I started finding myself in the word of God.

I surrounded myself with people who saw much more in me than I saw in myself. They pushed me to grow, which was painful because I had to confront all the lies about myself that I had believed for so long and had to do something about them.

It wasn't just that I didn't believe I could make an impact in this life, I didn't believe my life was worth anything. If you've ever felt that way or believed that about yourself, I am here to tell you that it is 100% NOT the truth.

Get ready because God is about to transform you.

Part of why I believed I was stupid was because I was really horrible at math. I had trouble reading numbers and understanding and retaining formulas. This wasn't something that I was ever formally diagnosed with while I was in school but, dyscalculia, a disorder much like dyslexia but with numbers, plagued me, and because it wasn't very severe it went unnoticed and I was just labeled as stupid and lazy.

Sometimes, there might be either a learning disability or a physical disability that traps you in those negative thoughts, but that doesn't define the spirit inside of you.

You need to take inventory of what I call your T.A.G.S.: Talents, Assets, Gifts and Skills. God has tagged you with some powerful things that you, and only you, have.

I didn't believe I had talent, but looking back to my childhood, I was always very vocal. I talked to anyone fearlessly, especially adults. I was loud, I was free and I was opinionated. That was my talent!

What changed?
After my family moved to another country, my accent and the way I spoke was foreign to everyone around me and I was made fun of.

My gift of speaking was attacked until I didn't want to talk to anyone anymore.

I used to command the attention of those around me but, because I was teased for the way I looked, I shrunk and wanted to just disappear, and I did. My once fearlessness was driven out of me until I had so many fears that I hid from my big dreams.

This was why I didn't believe I had anything of value to offer and believed what my father said, that we were not all created equal. I didn't have any faith that I could make a difference.

Things have changed because I started believing in who God said I was, that I am beautifully and wonderfully made—that I am His child and He has a plan and purpose for me. I started to see myself differently, started to uncover my talents and gifts; I started to shine.

No longer paying attention to those negative voices, I became a Best-Selling Author, writing this book to encourage you. I speak on stages sharing my message of confidence, I am an actor, have two businesses, a Podcast, and global Webshow that changes lives.

If I had continued to believe the lies of the Devil instead of looking at the T.A.G.S. that God bestowed upon me, I would have continued to see myself as a failure and continued to believe that I wasn't worth anything. I would not be here encouraging you to uncover your own unique Talents, Assets, Gifts and Skills so you can fulfill the plans God has for you stated in Jeremiah 29:11:

"For I know the plans I have for you," says the Lord. "They are plans for good and not for disaster, to give you hope and a future."

Go slay those negative thoughts and rise up with audacious confidence to all God has planned for you!

ALICIA COURI

About Alecia Couri: Alicia Couri, CEO of Audacious Concepts Inc., and founder of RedCarpetCEO™, is a multi-award-winning international & TEDx speaker, a Best-Selling Author, Business consultant and Legacy Queen for Woman of Achievement. She is passionate about empowering women to "own their awesome".

Author's Website: *www.AudaciousConceptsInc.Now.Site*

Book Series Website: *www.ThePrinciplesOfDebbieAndGoliath.com*

HABITS OF SUCCESS

AMY KEIDERLING
LOVE YOURSELF: BE-U-TIFUL GIRL!

I AM STRONG. I AM POWERFUL. I AM LOVE. I AM JOY. I AM ENOUGH. I AM UNIQUE. I AM CREATIVE. I AM SMART. I AM KIND. I AM INSPIRING. I AM CARING. I AM PASSIONATE. I AM ME!

I AM BE-U-TIFUL!

When I look at those empowering self-love statements, there was a time that I could barely type them out, let alone say them to myself or out loud. Today, it has taken me 50 years of life experiences, adventures, self-discovery, tears, laughter, growing pains, and joy to really know who I be. And the adventure continues...as so does yours.

When I was younger, my idol was WONDER WOMAN. She was tall, gorgeous, had beautiful dark hair, killer legs, an amazing costume, gold cuffs, a crown, red boots, an invisible jet, and the famous lasso of truth. She was strong, powerful, confident, beautiful, courageous, and stood for justice. She was everything that I wanted to be, yet never saw in myself. I had Wonder Woman dolls, PEZ dispensers, stickers, and t-shirts. I spent countless Halloweens dressing up for that one night to be Wonder Woman—in order to hide the real Amy and put on a mask and step powerfully into her red boots that made me stand taller and walk with authority and grace.

HABITS OF SUCCESS

Now, if you are wondering if I had an invisible jet, I did not, but I still to this day think that would be an epic gift. Not to mention the lasso of truth would have worked wonders over the years. Wonder Woman in my eyes had it all and as much as I longed to be her, I knew I would never be her.

You see, I was not like the other girls in my class. I was heavy, my parents were divorced, I didn't have the coolest trendiest clothes, I ran slow, didn't have a lot of friends, and I had short hair that my mom insisted on keeping in a Dorothy Hamil haircut. If you don't know who she is, just Google her. You will then feel my hair pain.

While all my girlfriends were getting awards like "prettiest girl," "best dressed," "cutest smile," "most popular," I was always left with the awards like "nicest girl." Yes, it is a great honor to be considered nice, but what I longed for was that Wonder Woman confidence, body, and power to show those classmates how truly wonderful I was. I was told by adults "at least you have a pretty face" or "you are just big boned." As much as they thought that they were supporting me, it only pushed me to hide my body, hate the person I saw in the mirror, and long to be someone I was not—BEAUTIFUL.

I have wasted so much time/energy/tears/worry and fear over the years wishing to be anyone but me. I spent so much time longing to be someone else, that I never got to really know me. What I discovered over the years is as much as I wanted to be Wonder Woman, I eventually found my own Wonder Woman inside me. Instead of focusing on all the things I hated about myself in the mirror, I started changing my mind and my words to start appreciating and honoring the amazing body that I was given. Was this easy? HECK NO! Did it take work? HECK YES! Is it something that I still work on today? ABSOLUTELY!

How did I start loving the girl in the mirror? I started really looking at her. I started seeing her. I stopped the voice in my head that told me she was not good enough, not beautiful enough, not funny enough, or just not enough. That voice in your head that talks down to you is one voice you can kindly tell to be quiet. Ask yourself—would you say those words to your best friend? NO! So, start being your own best friend! You see, the beautiful face you see in the mirror—there is NO ONE like you. You are unique. You are loved. You are enough.

I started seeing all the beautiful people around me, not for just how they looked on the outside, but for who they be on the inside. Their kindness, their love, their compassion, their giving, their humor, their laughter, their love that only they uniquely possess. When I started seeing the gifts in those around me, I started to see the gifts in myself.

I started writing on paper, post-it notes, stickers, and I even took lipstick on the bathroom mirror and wrote: BE-U-tiful GIRL! That's right! BE U! There is only one U! Honor her. Love her. Acknowledge her. It was daily reminders and encouragement to keep going that I eventually I found my inner Wonder Woman. I would say them out loud, even though it was very awkward at first. Seriously—I would stand in front of the mirror and whisper them so no one would hear. Each day it got a little bit easier. Then one day, I started to not only hear the words I was saying, but I also started to believe the words that I was saying. The beautiful girl you might be longing to be like—she is already inside you. Give her a hug, let her shine, and tell her that you are beautiful, loved and enough. Then one day I was shouting those words! AND I didn't care who heard me! I LOVE ME!

Create your own "I AM" statements. Write them on paper, stick them on your bathroom mirror, say them out loud, shout them to the stars, and truly believe with power and passion you are BE-U-tiful! Notice others around you, their beauty and acknowledge it. We can all lift each other up—for when I love me, I can truly see who you be.

Beauty comes from within—we get to start by loving ourselves first so we can love others around us. We can not truly love others to our fullest capacity if we are not loving ourselves with the same passion. This body that I spent 50 years hating and wishing and praying to be swapped out with Wonder Woman's body was never acknowledged or honored for all the gifts, adventures, joy, and memories we have created together.

This body has allowed me to run, dance, sing, laugh, cry, take adventures, hike, swim, ride rollercoasters, have children, survived sports injuries, skinned knees, bicycle accidents, celebrated life, fight cancer 3x, and has created 50 years of priceless memories that are mine. All these gifts my body has granted me are just as unique as I am. There is no one else like me! There is no one else like you! Imagine if we all looked the same. This would be a very boring world.

When you are longing to be someone you see, you are not honoring who you truly are. What if you looked in the mirror and fell in love with who you see? What if you thanked your beautiful body, mind, and spirit for gifting you each day to create memories and take adventures? What if we loved ourselves truly that we in turn can love others by seeing who they be?

Now, do I still love Wonder Woman? HECK YES! Do I still long for an invisible plane? HECK YES—as a girl can dream! Do I still get to tell myself these words every day? ABSOLUTELY!

I AM STRONG. I AM POWERFUL. I AM LOVE. I AM JOY. I AM ENOUGH. I AM UNIQUE. I AM CREATIVE. I AM SMART. I AM KIND. I AM INSPIRING. I AM CARING. I AM PASSIONATE. I AM ME!

I AM BE-U-TIFUL!

I AM AMY!

LIFE IS NOW! NOW IT IS YOUR TURN! "I AM...."

This book I dedicate to all the uniquely WONDER-ful Girls out there who may not love the face in the mirror. We see you! You are loved! You are beautiful! You are enough! We Got You!

LOVE YOURSELF: Be-U-tiful Girl!

AMY KEIDERLING

About Amy Keiderling: Amy Keiderling is a Rebel Soul Guide. She helps to navigate you to find your soul's purpose. Think of her as a co-pilot on the road of life. When the road gets bumpy, curvy, or just seems full of obstacles and detours, we will pull out our Rebel Roadmap and navigate it together.

Amy Keiderling is the owner of Modville, as well as an adventure guide with Modville Tours. Amy has always been an avid collector of anything vintage; the instant connection a piece gives you to a memory or story is why she loves her fab finds. Amy's passion grew stronger when she met Keith, as his passion for custom vintage cars, motorcycles, and random collectibles grew their collection. When Amy and Keith are not taking adventure lovers on chartered bus vacations or riding around on their motorcycles, you will find them lounging in Modville or out searching for another piece and their story. Amy encourages everyone to find their story, their fab finds, and adventures!

Author's Website: *www.ItsAMoAdventure.com*

Book Series Website: *www.ThePrinciplesofDebbieandGoliath.com*

HABITS OF SUCCESS

AZADEH BENNETT
A JOURNEY TO FREEDOM

We have so many Goliaths in this world. Some are known to us, while others remain unknown; until their shadow falls upon us. Some are visible to us long before we encounter them, while others remain invisible even after they've harmed us. The Goliaths faced by women of the world are hidden and have an impact deeper than the original in the story.

I was born and raised in Iran. You might have your own thoughts when you hear the country name Iran; I have lived in it for decades. When you are born somewhere you accept it to be your world. It is like you were born in a fish tank and that fish tank is your whole world.

However, our fish tank was set beside the ocean and I am so grateful to God for having a father opened my eyes about what is going on in the ocean rather than only inside our fish tank. My father is my role model to think differently. My father wished for me and my siblings to become scientists. Persian culture values education and science very much. My father and I usually talk about stars and how black holes are created and the galaxy or the construction of cells or molecules. When we craft a ring bell or some other electrical toy, my father explained every single structure of the electrical circuit so I understand how that craft works in detail. His wish was for me and my siblings to come abroad and become scientists or a university faculty that he believed would guarantee our future to be happy and successful. My father was the only spark of light inside of that fish tank.

HABITS OF SUCCESS

Goliath in the Society

However, there was a big Goliath in that fish tank. It was called Be Hushed Goliath! Other than my father, everything and everywhere else hushed us in that tank.

You might have heard of this saying in the United States, "Children should be seen and not heard." There is an old saying in Iran that goes, **"A good girl is a girl that has never been seen by the Sun or the Moon**." That means a good girl does not go out, contribute to society, and never speaks up. Though it is not applied literally as extreme as it sounds, you can imagine how that impacts a girl's life who wants to be accepted by family and society. I was that good girl!

That was what the Be Hushed Goliath's first impression to society. Be hushed! Never show up, express opinions, and speak up! Unlike my father, my mother promotes the norms of society with perfectionism. So, I was not speaking much around my mother and at home.

Goliath at Schools

The schools in Iran are separated by gender. The Goliath at schools commanded us to have loose, big, dark, and ugly uniforms at school. It also ruled that we girls should not have white shoes on at schools. We could not have nail polish and nobody should see our hair out of our big tied-up scarves around our head. Surely, we should not speak or laugh out loud that people on the other side of the school walls could hear us. Praise the Lord that our schoolyard was big enough that we could speak and laugh away from school walls. However, it did not stop us from sending out signs of our existence by high volleyball or basketball shots beyond the walls of the school to the boys' school nearby. Did I tell you that one of Goliath's rules for girls was that they should not contact, connect with, or communicate with any boys? Yes, it was/is.

Goliath in Religion

You might know that this Goliath was very religious too. He assigned all his rules according to his God's rules and commandments. And nobody could ask questions or question the Goliath's religion. There was one rule with his religion: This religion is the best and never ever ask a question about it. The Goliath's religion is all about fear, fear, fear, and weeping. If you want to go to heaven after death, you should fear his God to death and always be sad and cry all the time. No questions asked.

Goliath at work

Apply the same dress code for girls at school to women at work. Women should never get higher compensation than men because they are not officially responsible for the family.

Goliath at Court

If a woman gets arrested for having her hair out of her scarf or not having a scarf, she can face punishments that include up to two months in prison, fines of up to 500,000 rials and up to 74 lashes, and even dismissal from any job.

Women are worth half of a man. This means two women witnesses count as one man if they ever get the chance to be counted. A man can marry up to four women at one time; women can only marry one husband.

A woman could only get a divorce in court with a judge's order, while a man could get a divorce by declaring it verbally. A woman could not request for divorce unless she could prove to the court that her husband was imprisoned, mentally ill, physically abusive, or an addict. Even in that situation, there is no right for a woman to be awarded a divorce.
If a woman gets divorced, she might be preferential custody over children under seven. Courts determine whether a mother or father gets custody of children older than seven. A divorced woman forfeits child custody if she remarries, even if her husband is dead.

A woman could not work outside of her home, travel, and go to university without permission from her husband, father, uncle, or the patriarch of the family. A widower inherits his wife's entire estate while a widow only inherits one-eighth of her husband's estate. Goliath hushed everyone who questioned these rights over women of the society.

HABITS OF SUCCESS

Beyond the Fish Tank

Goliath in my homeland is so big that its shadow not only covers all over my homeland but also comes out of the borders and ruins other places too. I admit that I did not see the power in me to fight this Goliath when I was living under his shadow. Therefore, I came out of his shadow, and the fish tank to the ocean. Fishes in that tank raised and shouted out to the Goliath that we do not want him and asked for help and support from the ocean outside. Now I can see clearly how big is this Goliath. I see that fishes in the tank cannot kill this Goliath and get free by themselves. Now I have a mission to inform everybody and anybody that I can about this Goliath who kills my people and he never feels full of drinking my people's blood.

A Call for Unity

I urge you to join me and my people in standing against this giant in Iran. You have Kings in your land that have killed their Goliath. Please let your kings know that all the ocean needs to unite to conquer against this Goliath that will come after you and your land and your kingdom when he kills all the fish of that fish tank. This Goliath will not die by the effort of one Debbie or a David. Let's take him down all together.

To be continued...

AZADEH BENNETT

About Azadeh Bennett: Azadeh Bennett, a remarkable advocate for "woman life freedom," champions the rights of women in Iran and across the globe, advocating for the freedom they deserve. Azadeh Bennett is, also, a Strategic Communication and Leadership consultant, dedicated to empowering organizations and executives to reach their full potential. With master's degrees in MBA, Strategic Communication, and Global Studies, she has become a transformational coach, and executive mentor, dedicating her life to empowering others on their journey to personal and professional transformation.

In addition to her professional pursuits, Azadeh finds solace in nature through hiking, expresses her creativity by playing the harp, and channels her artistic spirit into acrylic painting. Her commitment to creativity, leadership, freedom, and communication extends to her work with individuals and organizations. Azadeh's unwavering dedication is further enriched by her loving marriage to Jason Bennett, whose unwavering support fuels her passion for transformation and freedom. Together, they stand as a testament to the power of love and partnership in pursuing God in one's life purpose.

Azadeh's driving force is to equip individuals and businesses with the tools to excel and create a positive impact on the world. She firmly believes in the power of love, freedom, communication, and connection as vehicles for fostering a better place to live. Through her expertise and guidance, she aspires to uplift professionals and organizations, steering them to the pinnacle of success. Learn more about her services at *CreativeLeadershipco.com*.

Author's Website: *www.AzadehBennett.com*
Book Series Website: *www.ThePrinciplesOfDebbieAndGoliath.com*

HABITS OF SUCCESS

DR. BETTY SPEAKS
NAVIGATING LIFE'S STORMS WITH RESILIENCE AND DIVINE AUTHORITY

Life, as I've come to understand it, is a journey filled with ebbs and flows, much like the palm trees I so dearly admire. These trees, with their remarkable resilience, bend in the storm but always return upright, never losing a leaf. My journey, akin to these steadfast trees, has been a testament to resilience, faith, and divine guidance.

As I reflect on my journey, through the various phases of my life, I recognize that each phase is marked by its unique challenges and learnings. I delved into the depths of personal development, the essence of coping mechanisms, and the paramount importance of staying anchored in life's tumultuous seas.

I often recall the words of Winston Churchill, "Never, never give up." These words resonate deeply with me, serving as a beacon through my trials. Like many, I've had my share of falling into metaphorical wells. But before each fall, I've learned to tie a rope around a sturdy tree, ensuring that I can pull myself back out. This rope symbolizes my coping mechanisms: self-care, meditation, and surrounding myself with like-minded individuals who reinforce my positivity and resilience.

HABITS OF SUCCESS

Self-care, to me, is not just a practice; it's a pilgrimage. I've found solace in retreating into my wilderness, a space for meditation and contemplation, which allows me to re-emerge stronger and more centered. In these moments of solitude, I'm reminded of the words from Psalms 92:12, "Still, I rise." These words are a powerful affirmation of my resilience, mirroring the unyielding spirit of the palm tree that weathers the storm and stands tall in its aftermath.

My life's journey has been a tapestry woven with experiences of personal challenges and triumphs. Growing up in a complex family situation, I learned early the significance of personal resilience and staying true to oneself. I've navigated through whispers and judgments, always conscious of the choices before me. These experiences taught me the importance of reacting to situations not with bitterness, but with understanding and grace.

Recent reflections brought to light the profound truth of preparation in life. My upbringing, particularly under the guidance of my grandmother, instilled in me a deep connection with divine authority. The story of Jesus carrying his cross, enduring ridicule and obstacles, is a poignant reminder of the inevitability of stumbling blocks in our lives. It's through these narratives that I've learned the essence of walking in divine authority and preparing for the unknown.

Leadership, a role I've embraced in various facets of my life, demands this preparation and understanding of divine authority. To lead is to walk fearlessly, carrying within oneself a divine authority that guides and prepares us for challenges. In my journey, prayer and self-awareness have been instrumental in fortifying this divine authority. It's about knowing who I am in Him and who He is in me, allowing me to engage effectively with the world around me.

Life today presents a myriad of challenges, and as leaders, we must maintain our peace and purpose amidst these trials. My experiences, the training I've received, and the encounters I've had, all converge to shape the leader I am today—one who walks in divine purpose, guided by divinity itself.

THE PRINCIPLES OF DEBBIE & GOLIATH

And in those moments of solitude, much like Christ in the wilderness, I find the strength to prepare for the tasks ahead. This private time is essential, not only for reflection but for equipping oneself with the armor needed to face life's battles.

And so, here I am, sharing my journey, hoping that my words will resonate with those who find themselves amidst life's tempests, reminding them that resilience, anchored in divine authority, is the key to not just enduring but triumphing over life's challenges.

Reflecting back on my journey, I realize that each step, each stumble, has been instrumental in shaping the person I am today. A significant part of this journey has been learning to embrace and understand the complexity of my family dynamics. Being the only child from my parents, yet having half-siblings from their subsequent marriages, presented its unique set of challenges. It was a world filled with diverse perspectives, often accompanied by whispers and unspoken judgments. However, these very experiences honed my ability to empathize, to see beyond the surface, and to understand the underlying emotions and motivations of those around me.

One of the most profound lessons I learned during these formative years was the power of choice. The ability to choose one's response to any situation is a powerful tool. I remember times when I felt alienated, times when whispers would cease as I entered a room, leaving a palpable tension in the air. It was during these moments I realized that I had the power to choose my response. I could either let these situations embitter me or use them as steppingstones to build resilience and understanding. I chose the latter.

This lesson of choice and resilience was not just theoretical but was tested in real-life situations. One such instance occurred during my teenage years. I encountered what we now recognize as bullying, a concept that was not as clearly defined back then. Despite the hurt and confusion it caused, I chose to respond with kindness and understanding. It's fascinating how life unfolds; the very person who once bullied me is now a dear friend. This transformation was possible because I chose not to let their actions define me, but rather to respond with the goodness and righteousness that I believed were inherent in me.

My faith has been the cornerstone of my journey. I often reflect on the biblical story of Jesus carrying his cross, a narrative that vividly illustrates the concept of preparation and divine authority. This story has been a source of strength and inspiration, particularly in times of adversity. It serves as a reminder that life will inevitably present us with challenges, but it is our preparation, both spiritual and mental, that equips us to face these challenges with grace and resilience.

This preparation is not just about facing adversities; it's also about stepping into leadership roles. As a leader, I've learned that one must walk in divine authority, carrying within oneself a confidence and fearlessness that can only come from a deep spiritual grounding. This authority is not about exerting power over others but about being a guiding light, a source of inspiration and strength to those we lead. It's about leading with empathy, understanding, and a steadfast commitment to our values and purpose.

Leadership, in my experience, is also about maintaining peace in the midst of challenges. This peace is not merely the absence of conflict but a state of inner calm and clarity that allows us to navigate through storms without losing sight of our purpose. It's about being an example to others, showing them that it is possible to face adversity with grace and emerge stronger on the other side.

Personal development has been another key aspect of my journey. It's a continuous process of self-reflection, learning, and growth. I've found that surrounding myself with like-minded individuals, engaging in self-care practices, and staying connected to my spiritual roots have been pivotal in my personal growth. These practices have not only helped me bounce back from difficult situations but have also enabled me to evolve and adapt, much like the palm tree that bends in the storm but never breaks.

As I share these reflections, I am reminded of the importance of doing good irrespective of the circumstances we face. It's a principle I hold dear and strive to live by. Doing good, being kind, and living righteously are not just moral choices; they are a reflection of the divine essence within us. They are what enable us to rise above challenges, to transform adversity into opportunity, and to be a beacon of hope and inspiration to others.

In closing, I want to emphasize the importance of preparation, both in facing life's challenges and in stepping into leadership roles. Preparation, in my view, is not just about acquiring knowledge or skills; it's about cultivating a mindset, a way of being that is rooted in divine authority, resilience, and a commitment to doing good. It's about walking in our purpose, guided by our values and faith, and being a source of strength and inspiration to those around us.

As I continue on this journey, I am ever mindful of the lessons learned, the challenges overcome, and the wisdom gained. My hope is that my story, my reflections, will resonate with you, offering guidance, inspiration, and a reminder that no matter what storms you may face, you have the strength and the divine authority to rise above them and emerge stronger and more resilient.

HABITS OF SUCCESS

DR. BETTY SPEAKS

About Dr. Betty Speaks: Dr. Speaks is a United States Army retiree, the CEO of A Life Change NOW, and Podcast Host of Overcoming Battles by Being Strong and Courageous. The Artist/Songwriter of the Single "It's A Resurrection. She is your Lifetime IMPRINT EMPRESS! She is very passionate about MOTIVATING individuals to resurrect and establish themselves spiritually, personally, or professionally. She's that chosen warrior who inspires others to create A Life Change Now by leaving an INTENTIONAL IMPACTFUL IMPRINT for INFINITY. Betty is extremely passionate about helping individuals establish themselves and their generational wealth via multiple streams of income plus securing their retirement endeavors. She also mentors youthful ladies and other individuals or teams during Transformational Workshops or One-On-One Mentorship, and other Total Well-Being Events. Betty Speaks… "IT" When She Speaks. As an independent artist and songwriter, Dr. Betty Speaks is on a mission to share her transformative international leadership song, "It's A Resurrection." With a desire to reach a global audience, she uses her creative expression to inspire positive change worldwide. Dr. Speaks acknowledges the profound impact women have had on shaping the world for way over 200 years. "It's A Resurrection" serves as more than just a song; it's an opportunity for her to provide testimony from a leader's perspective. She conveys the message that, despite life's most challenging endeavors, she can conquer and resurrect to lead because He's alive in her. Dr. Betty Speaks invites listeners to embrace the powerful narrative where the melody becomes a testament to her resilience and leadership. Through this song, she aims to spread the message of triumph over challenges and the ability to emerge stronger, echoing the resurrection theme in both life and leadership.

Author's Website: *www.BettySpeaks.com*
Book Series Website: *www.ThePrinciplesOfDebbieAndGoliath.com*

THE PRINCIPLES OF DEBBIE & GOLIATH

HABITS OF SUCCESS

THE PRINCIPLES OF DEBBIE & GOLIATH

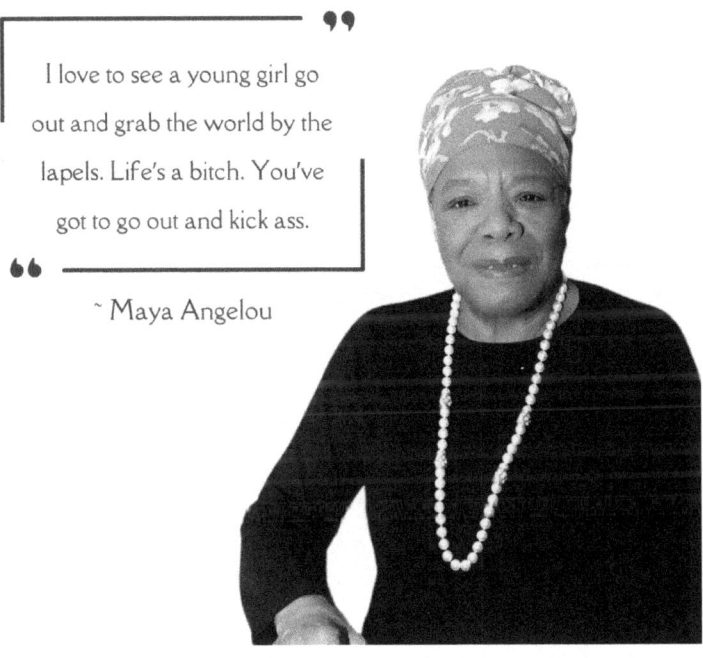

> I love to see a young girl go out and grab the world by the lapels. Life's a bitch. You've got to go out and kick ass.
>
> ~ Maya Angelou

HABITS OF SUCCESS

CHARLOTTE DELON
WORK ON ME

It is said that we become the sum of our experiences from 0-18 years of age. From elementary school through high school, I was bullied. I honestly believe I got bullied because I had my own mind. I was never a follower. My mom always said, "You march to the beat of your own drum and if you ever get in trouble, I will know it's because you chose."

I came across a diary from when I was around 16 or 17 years old, and it saddened me. I don't remember writing the words, but I was talking about how I no longer wanted to live. I shared my diary with my children because I wanted them to know we all have moments of weakness and if they ever had the thought, I didn't want them to think they were alone, or I couldn't relate. I thank God that I never acted on it because today I'm grateful that I'm still here and I know whatever comes my way I can handle it.

The main thing that I learned from dealing with bullies for most of my life is they try to find vulnerabilities and exploit them. Bullies can come in any shape, age, or size. One of my bullies was a high school guidance counselor. I was in the sewing room and the counselor came in and scowled at me and said, "You are pretty, and you know it." It was code for conceited. Truthfully, I didn't think I was pretty. Not even a little.

I didn't respond. I didn't know what to say to the statement. I put my head down and began to walk away. My favorite teacher pulled me over and said, "Hold your head up. You don't allow anyone to make you feel bad about yourself." Those words were cemented in my brain.

HABITS OF SUCCESS

As I continued to go through life, I realized the bullies didn't go away, they just appeared different. They are all adults now. In deep reflection, I began to ponder what it was about me that attracted bullies. I thought, I'm kind. I'm inclusive. I try to make sure everyone feels loved when in my space. Why do I attract bullies? I wondered what I was projecting into the world that would attract these kinds of people to me.

Then, I was told I'm light in darkness. It's simple. Darkness is attracted to light. I'm not causing these people to come into my life. It's kind of like bad boys are attracted to good girls. I call these people the light dimmers. If you don't understand your superpowers and you are not grounded in your genius, light dimmers can cause you not to live in your purpose. They will put your light out.

As I grew and matured, I had to identify my Goliaths if I was going to slay them—not just for me, but for others. Most times, we have no idea that we are empowering the Goliaths around us and giving them life. Here are steps used to slay my Goliath.

- **PAY ATTENTION TO THE INNER CRITIC.** My inner critic gave my Goliaths power. Why? Because I believed the negative self-talk. Our minds are like our closet. We need to occasionally take inventory and purge some of the old to make room for the new. Our minds are no different. It takes the same amount of energy to have negative thoughts as there is positive. An exercise that works is when you have a thought ask yourself is this thought helping or hurting? If you believe the thought is hurting, choose a new thought. This is a muscle, but I promise if you exercise it, you will experience major shifts in your life.

Another strategy to silencing your inner critic is to put a thin rubber band on your arm and when you catch yourself having negative self-talk, you pop yourself—not with the intent to hurt, but to disrupt your negative thinking.

- **BE CAREFUL OF GROUP THINK.** I tell my kids a quote by Dr. Suess, "Why try to fit in when you were born to stand out?" We spend so much of our time trying to be like everyone else that we deprive the world of who we are. "Group think" is a major component of a bullying experience. Following the crowd can make you bully people. "Group think" behavior is an indicator that you do not feel safe to stand out. Lean into courage and respect your mind and your values. There is nothing more suffocating than not being able to be your authentic self. I think back to my high school days where I lost friends because I had my own thoughts and they tried to pressure me into thinking and believing like them. I felt if they were truly my friends, they would have respected my individuality. To follow others means we are dishonoring our own geniuses.

- **FIND YOUR VOICE.** As a female, it is critical to have an opinion. I grew up learning I was to be seen and not heard. I had opinions that I often kept to myself. I remember thinking I wanted to be invisible, thinking it would make my bullies go away. It actually causes the bullies to focus on you.

Through my experiences, I was able to help my daughter navigate her bullies. She was in the second or third grade and had a run in with bullies. I sent her to school with an Afro. She looked so pretty. These girls approached her and said in a disapproving way, "Your hair," teasing about her Afro. I asked my daughter, "What did you do?" and she said, "I put my hood on and went outside." I said, "Oh no! You just gave your bullies power, and they are going to bully you again tomorrow. But don't worry, you will be ready."

I told her, when they approach you say, "What!" with a strong and powerful voice. You want to attract the teachers for them to wonder what is going on. At first, she said "What" in a very wimpy voice. I said, "You are not going to scare anyone with that voice." We practiced until she was powerful. Just as I said, the bullies approached her again. She said in a very strong voice, "What!" and startled her bullies. They responded, "Nothing. We just wanted to say your hair is nice." They never messed with her again. Today, my daughter is 22 and she's strong and powerful and advocates for herself while she navigates college.

HABITS OF SUCCESS

- **EMBRACE YOU.** I'm tall and while I embrace it now and love it, there was a time when I felt it was a curse. Imagine being in elementary school and towering over everyone. I was tall, gangly, and timid. I remember telling my mom, "What's the point of a pretty dress? No one is going to see it." I was always in the back row because of my height. I was constantly teased because I was different.

As I grew older, in my upper teens, I chose to embrace my difference and do it with intention. I started modeling. I found my niche that was specific to tall women. I never went professional, but I started to appreciate my height and feel pretty. Because I grew up feeling awkward about my height for a long time, I made sure to put my daughter into activities for tall women. She played basketball, volleyball, and fencing. She once said she wanted to be over 6 feet and I smiled. She almost achieved it. She's 5'11". I love my height and she loves hers. She and I get to be over 6 feet when we wear our heels together. Remember, you are uniquely and wonderfully made!

While it was a journey and one that I do not regret, now I know and love myself. I understand my superpowers and I'm grounded in my genius. I hope this helps you to slay your Goliaths and step into your genius.

CHARLOTTE DELON

About Charlotte DeLon: Charlotte is a motivational speaker and coach with over 16 years of transformational leadership experience. She helps organizations transform culture for optimal output defining operational tenants and assessing behavioral gaps that can impede or accelerate change.

Charlotte is a Maxwell Leadership Certified Team Member and Certified Advance Behavioral Analysis DISC coach. Through the discovery of DISC results, Charlotte helps individuals define their superpowers and also what can be holding them back from being all that is possible.

Speaking: Keynote speaker, panel discussions for women in IT providing strategies on how to manage work, family and life, launched leader to leader series discussing Leadership Philosophy's and benefits.

Coaching: Executive leadership coaching to improve organizational health. Career and life coach helping people succeed in career and managing life challenges like fear.

Teaching: Facilitate Leadership Acumen Mastermind series. Train on leadership styles (situational, transformational and servant). Teach how to build Leadership Philosophy's to deliver and drive inner and outer accountability.

Favorite Quote: *"No one cares how much you know until they know how much you care."* ~ Theodore Roosevelt.

Author's Website: *www.LeadershipByCharlotteDelon.com*
Book Series Website: *www.ThePrinciplesOfDebbieAndGoliath.com*

HABITS OF SUCCESS

CYNTHIA GALLARDO
BEYOND YOUR GOLIATH: THE LEGACY OF SYNERGY

In the vast tapestry of human endeavor, each thread, each story, weaves into the next, creating a pattern far greater than the sum of its parts. This chapter is dedicated to young women around the world, to inspire you to move beyond your personal Goliaths and embrace the power of legacy and synergy.

I. Understanding Your Goliath

Every young woman faces her own Goliath. This metaphorical giant represents the fears, doubts, and societal pressures that can hold you back. It's the voice that whispers, "You can't," when your heart screams, "I can." Recognizing your Goliath is the first step in overcoming it. Understand that these fears are common; they don't diminish your potential. Instead, they offer a chance to grow.

Defeating your Goliath is a continuous work in progress. I was once that young girl facing myself, my own Goliath. With many challenges and lessons learned, I pushed forward successfully. I continue to forge my way forward because with each new chapter in my life, comes a new Goliath that I must overcome. Never stop fighting and keep moving forward.

HABITS OF SUCCESS

II. Legacy: The Strength of Stories

The concept of legacy is powerful. It's not just about what we leave behind, but what we build upon. The stories of women who came before us—their struggles, triumphs, and lessons—are not just tales of the past. They are guideposts and sources of strength. Read about women in science, arts, politics, and other fields who defied their own Goliaths. Draw inspiration from their journeys, knowing that their legacies are not their achievements alone, but also the paths they paved for you.

I am personally grateful and give thanks to those who have paved the way for me, and it is a privilege to pave the way for other young girls and women that come behind me. I gladly step aside to allow each of you to catapult forward. We are in this together!

III. Synergy: The Magic of Collaboration

Synergy occurs when individuals come together, and their combined efforts create something greater. It's about harnessing the power of 'we' instead of just 'I.' In your journey, seek out mentors, peers, and communities. Collaborate, share, and learn from each other. Remember, synergy is not just about working together; it's about resonating together, where your collective energy amplifies your individual strengths.

I clearly remember that I almost let my Goliath win because I was so close to quitting law school several times. Synergy saved me. I had a law professor who made this statement during class one day, "You can only give your reasonable best." That statement lifted a self-created load from my shoulders. I didn't have to be the best, I just had to survive and make it through law school. I am proud to say that by giving my reasonable best at all times, I graduated with honors. For someone who consistently had the though of quitting law school at top of mind, I can say with confidence that I slayed my Goliath. If I can do it, you can, too!

IV. Breaking Down the Walls

Your Goliath may seem invincible, but remember, walls can be climbed, tunneled under, or walked around. Be creative in your approach.

THE PRINCIPLES OF DEBBIE & GOLIATH

Sometimes, moving forward means taking a step back to reassess and strategize. It's okay to feel overwhelmed; what's important is not to let that stop you. Seek out different perspectives and be open to unconventional solutions.

I was an unconventional law student because I attended law school later in life as a career change. I have always been passionate about helping others. I chose to do so in a different profession. I attended law school part-time while being a wife, mother, foster parent, and entrepreneur. Don't let your Goliath defeat you!

V. Embracing Failure as a Stepping Stone

In your journey, you will face setbacks. Embrace them. Each failure is a lesson, an integral part of your growth. It's in these moments that resilience is forged. Resilience isn't about not falling; it's about knowing how to get back up. Each time you rise, you do so stronger, wiser, and more determined.

I have suffered many failures. I have fallen many times. I have experienced defeat. I will admit, I did wallow in my sorrows for a moment; yet, ultimately and with help, I didn't let that stop me. I continued forward on those stepping stones that my past failures created.

VI. The Power of Self-Belief

Believe in yourself. This simple yet profound act is revolutionary. Your belief is the slingshot that can bring down your Goliath. It starts with changing the narrative in your mind from "I can't" to "I will." Self-belief is a muscle—the more you use it, the stronger it gets.

Let's use that muscle together!

VII. Setting Goals and Taking Action

Dreams are essential, but without action, they remain just that – dreams. Set tangible goals. Break them down into achievable steps. Celebrate each small victory, for they are the steps that lead to great achievements. Remember, the journey of a thousand miles begins with a single step.

A key part of my personal creed is results not excuses. Also, if you have a problem, create a solution. The only way to achieve results and to create a solution is by setting goals and taking action. You can do this!

VIII. Nurturing Your Inner Circle

Surround yourself with people who believe in you and your vision. This inner circle will be your support system, your sounding board, and sometimes, your reality check. They are an integral part of your synergy circle. Cultivate these relationships with care and reciprocity.

I appreciate my inner circle that has helped me in so many ways in all areas of my life. Your inner circle can do the same.

IX. The Importance of Self-Care

In your journey to conquer Goliath, don't forget to take care of yourself. Self-care is not selfish; it's essential. It ensures that you are at your best, physically, mentally, emotionally, and spiritually. This includes rest, hobbies, and time for reflection. A well-rested mind is a powerful tool.

I created and live by the Legacypreneur™ Blueprint that includes the following steps: 1. **S**ave **Y**ourself, 2. **N**ext **E**veryone Else, 3. **R**eassess/Repeat, 4. **G**ive, and 5. **Y**es! Yes! Yes! (Celebrate).

Save yourself involves self-care. You can't help anyone ese if you don't save yourself first. Think of an emergency on an airplane, the oxygen mask goes on you first so that you can later help others.

X. Paying It Forward

As you move forward, remember to look back and extend a hand to those following in your footsteps. Mentor, guide, and inspire. Your journey can light the way for others. This is how you build your legacy—not just through your achievements, but by uplifting others.

With this chapter, I endeavor to pay it forward and share with you to empower you to continue forward by defeating your Goliath.

Conclusion: The Journey Ahead

Your journey will be unique, filled with highs and lows. But remember, each step forward, no matter how small, is a victory over your Goliath. Embrace the legacy of the women who walked before you and build on it. Create synergy by working with others who share your vision. Together, you can turn the impossible into the possible.

As you close this chapter, remember that your story is just beginning. You are not just facing your Goliath; you are moving beyond it, creating a legacy of strength, collaboration, and endless possibilities. The world is waiting for your contribution. Go forth with courage, determination, and the knowledge that you are not alone in this journey.

Author's Note: This chapter is an invitation to dream, dare, and do. It's a call to young women everywhere to rise above their fears, harness the collective power of synergy, and build a legacy that resonates through generations. Remember, you are the author of your story, and every page you turn is a step towards a future where the impossible becomes possible.

CYNTHIA GALLARDO

About Cynthia Gallardo: Cynthia Gallardo, your Leading Legacy Lawyer™, is keynote speaker, author, business strategist, legacypreneur™, and lawyer. Cynthia is passionate about providing a positive interaction with every person she meets on a daily basis, whether in a personal, professional, or academic setting. Cynthia's creed is "Results. Not excuses." Cynthia is a catalyst that empowers and inspires entrepreneurs struggling to transform a business idea to a vision to a reality to a profitable business by discovering their unique business DNA to launch, build, and protect their legacy. Cynthia graduated with honors earning her MBA and law degree. Cynthia is a proud graduate of Southern University Law Center. Cynthia is CEO and founder of Cynthia Gallardo Law, LLC and Synergy Solutions PRO, LLC which houses Launch to Legacy Academy™. Cynthia practices immigration law, transactional law, and estate planning. Cynthia takes a holistic approach to business and shares her 5 Step Launch to Legacy™ Blueprint outlining the framework to live and leave a lasting legacy. Cynthia worked in the corporate environment for nearly fifteen years transitioning from front-line representative to management roles to a leadership role. Cynthia is a lifelong learner and strives to guide others to become the best versions of themselves personally and professionally.

Cynthia lives in Louisiana with her husband and son where they enjoy spending time together in spiritual activities. In addition, the Gallardo family has four furbabies – three Doberman pinschers and a cat. The Gallardo family is a strong advocate of the foster-to-adoption program as they have personally taken the foster-to-adoption journey.

Author's Website: *www.CynthiaGallardo.com*

Book Series Website: *www.ThePrinciplesOfDebbieAndGoliath.com*

DEBORAH J. ANDERSON
WHO DO YOU CHOOSE TO FOLLOW?

"Follow me where I go, what I do and who I know. Make it part of you to be a part of me... Take my hand and say you'll follow me." John Denver was an iconic musician in the 1970s who wrote approximately three hundred songs about self-awareness, nature, and love. The song, Follow Me, was inspired by his strong desire to travel and seek adventure, discover new things that lied ahead, and getting outside of his comfort zone as he explored the world. His song suggests one should be open to new experiences, and that some things are worth following. Following our heart, taking risks, trusting those we love, and seeking adventure are beautiful ways in which we can express our true identity, who we truly are.

As a pre-teen or teen, "Follow me" might look very different from exploring nature or traveling around the country. It probably shows up in the form of dressing like others and listening to pop culture music. Motivational speakers might encourage us to get outside of our comfort zone and take risks, but, as a young teen, these risks might include drinking alcohol and using drugs, or driving erratically, maybe even under the influence. Cheating on an exam, shop lifting and stealing are ways that many teens take risks as they follow their 'popular' friends and peers.

HABITS OF SUCCESS

The lives of young teens are filled with lots of noise and distractions. Celebrities and actors, pop culture singers and popular influencers on social media are idolized. Performances in sports and academics determines one's self-worth. So much importance is placed on Facebook likes and the number of subscribers we have on YouTube or TikTok. Eventually, along the way we discover life isn't portrayed accurately by the photos and events posted on social media, which includes the ability to edit or even delete.

There's also the noise we hear coming from the voices of others: parents, teachers, coaches, friends, and boyfriends. We don't know who we are and far too often create our self-identity based upon the feedback we hear, sometimes selectively, from the voice of public opinion.

If we are blessed, we will learn to develop a self-identity that comes from the voices of genuine kindness and positive attention we receive from others who have a true portrait of us. We take on an identity that does not come from ill-intentioned opinions or distorted verdicts of others, but rather, an identity that helps us to determine our judgments and values, our purpose and mission for our life. We keep searching and searching, and yet, we just don't see through the fog, or the distractions when we are seeking comfort, socialization, and material things. What we want we already have, and it won't be found in friendships, relationships, jobs, money, sports, or college.

As I reflect on my teen years, I recognize I was not a follower. There was a voice I listened to, however, a very strong and destructive voice, and it was not that of my friends and peer group. In my attempt to be a good girl, I didn't drink, or use drugs. I maintained excellent grades and was very active in junior high and high school, had a lot of great friends, and loved school.

It was through school I found my identity—an identity that would lead to my career decisions and much success in my work. Teachers, counselors, and administrators, as well as university professors were kind, supportive, encouraging, and affirmed for me who I was; friendly, intelligent, and a leader. However, the 'other' voices I heard early in my childhood are the voices that put me on a path of desperately wanting to please others, desperately wanting to be loved, and codependent. I'd find this path to be one of ongoing failure, and one that took decades to resolve. I found some*one* to follow that completely changed my life, and was an answer to prayer.

Before I would be led by this some*one,* I spent decades following others; not by duplicating their behaviors or participating in the same types of activities. I managed to stay away from some very common and typical teen activities that are illegal and potentially dangerous. As "Debbie" I had a good girl image to uphold, and I did it very well. The destructive path would begin when "Deb" was looking in all the wrong places for love and following all the wrong people.

We are encouraged to dream and create goals for our lives. As two very distinct paths emerged in my life, I found it easy to dream and create goals for one of those paths. The other path, I didn't create dreams or goals. In fact, at an early age I was highly discouraged from doing so. The voices I heard at home and the way in which I would identify myself was not one of kindness, support, encouragement, or love. My home environment was one where there was little or no communication, being teased and called names, where dreaming was "crazy," or wanting to do something fun was "goofy."

"Debbie" was my preferred name as a child. I dreamed of becoming a drum majorette, having watched my aunt lead the marching band in her high school. This dream wasn't discouraged (nor was it encouraged), and I kept my hopes to myself for approximately ten years. Entering high school as a sophomore, I tried out for the marching band and made it! I was so incredibly excited and I fully enjoyed being the lead drum majorette throughout high school.

To this day, I remember it being the one and only dream I would have as a child and one that was fulfilled. In time, when I started following that some*one*, I learned to never doubt the power of a dream and my ability to achieve that dream. Our most unbelievable dreams can be achieved, as long as we believe.

Over time, I became known as "Deb." I studied to become a special education teacher and my career included many great opportunities. A failed first marriage leading to divorce opened up the opportunity to teach as a professor at a state university. It was there that again I would experience the kindness, support, and encouragement of my Department Head. He had planted a seed and insisted I consider working on my doctorate. It was several decades later, but, in time, I did complete a doctoral program in Educational Administration and again experienced the fulfillment of a dream. It was the planting of the seed and knowing someone believed in me and saw the possibilities more than I could or would see for myself that filled my heart.

As I reflect back on a period of time in my life when I was "Deb," despite many successes in my career and now having two amazing boys, I was being a follower. It looked something like shadowing, but not as a job opportunity, seeking to determine if this job or that job would be a good fit for me. No, I was shadowing peers who drank, smoked, swore, and did a lot of inappropriate stuff. Even attending church only on a Sunday morning was not part of the lifestyle at that time. I managed not to participate in those behaviors but, I still followed, maybe subconsciously wanting to fit in and be accepted; to be loved by someone, even if they were the wrong set of peers. I had developed a form of codependency that would impact my life for many decades.

All of my work, like school, was enjoyable to me. Many opportunities emerged and doors opened as I left teaching to become a special education administrator and university professor. Relationships, however, were one failed moment after another. The shadowing of all the wrong people, looking for acceptance in the wrong places, wanting to be loved by the wrong people, was my desperate search to find myself. I just kept looking in the wrong places with the wrong individuals. Unlike my work, in my personal life I did not know or understand my core values, I didn't have the courage to stand up for what I believed in. I sat on the sidelines, not fully understanding I had fallen victim to my lack of identity or self-worth.

My "Goliath" moment would come but not yet. In time "Deborah" would emerge and rise up through a tremendous amount of hurt, pain, and loss.

THE PRINCIPLES OF DEBBIE & GOLIATH

When others had believed in me before, I would now believe in myself. I would not just sit on the sideline, but I literally would get in the 'game' and say, "Yes," to all the possibilities that laid before me. I would be made whole. I would find freedom, along with a deep sense of peace and joy despite my outer circumstances. When we not only believe, stop following the wrong people and things, and are called to follow Christ our lives change. God would put a Goliath moment in my life, and I would find the Deborah within.

DR. DEBORAH J. ANDERSON

About Dr. Deborah J. Anderson: Dr. Deborah J. Anderson has worked as a special education teacher, administrator, and university professor. As a professional speaker, life coach, and author, Deborah inspires others to achieve a higher level of success through maximum productivity, action, and capitalizing on one's strengths. Deborah resides in her home state of Nebraska, where she has used her retirement as an opportunity to "refire:" serving others through various ministries. She serves as the Team Lead in Omaha for God's Bucket Brigade, blessing and loving the homeless with help for today, and hope for tomorrow. In addition, she leads and facilitates Fresh Start groups for women who are experiencing the effects of offense, hurt, and loss through the transforming power of Jesus. Deborah is going ALL IN and saying, "Yes" to whatever God is calling her to do. Deborah is dedicating this chapter to two of her granddaughters, Reagan and Kennedy.

Author's Website: *www.LinkedIn.com/in/Dr-Deborah-J-Anderson*

Book Series Website: *www.ThePrinciplesOfDebbieAndGoliath.com*

ELAINE R. SUGIMURA
WHAT MAKES LIFE MEANINGFUL

"Challenges are what make life interesting. Overcoming them is what makes life meaningful."

~ Joshua J. Marine

ELAINE R. SUGIMURA

About Elaine R. Sugimura: Elaine is an accomplished CEO turned Business Consultant / Life Strategist who has a passion for creating Leaders amongst Leaders. With over 35+ years in the fashion and food and beverage industry, she has a passion to not only lead but support those who are seeking to reinvent who they are no matter where they are in life. She is a two-time breast cancer survivor and she knows a thing or two about surviving to thriving. Fun fact: she is an adrenaline junkie —the higher, the faster, the better. Her love for adventure has led her to travel to many parts of the world by plane, train and automobile. She and her husband, Hiro, share their home in Northern California. They have raised two extraordinary sons, Bryce and Cole and have added two beautiful daughters-in-law, Erica and Giselle to their growing family. Her legacy is to share what is possible when we open ourselves up to the issues that hold us back. Her Life's mission is to move those who are just surviving into Thrivers!

Author's Website: *www.ElaineRSugimura.co*m

Book Series Website: *www.ThePrinciplesOfDebbieAndGoliath.com*

EILEEN E. GALBRAITH
MENTORSHIP TO SUCCESS

In the bustling city of Prospera, there lived a determined woman named Eileen. Despite her unwavering spirit, Eileen found herself entangled in the complex web of financial struggles. As a single woman, she juggled the demands of her job while striving to provide a comfortable life for herself and two furry friends, Zeus and Cleo.

Eileen's financial challenges stemmed from an unexpected divorce, hence her being single again, increased expenses, mounting debts, and a lack of financial literacy. However, she refused to be defined by her difficulties. Instead, she saw them as steppingstones to a better future.

While navigating an unplanned personal bankruptcy, Eileen came to realize there were certain steps that she embarked upon which led to many fascinating people and discoveries.

As women, we tend to allow ourselves to let the energy and emotions that we have around money drag us down, instead of lifting us up. Eileen's Journey took her on a remarkable discovery. Yes, money does have energy and, yes, there is an emotional side to how we view it.

What follows are simple steps all women can take, just like Eileen did, to come into their full potential in their personal and business lives. Follow along and you, too, will create financial bliss in your life, just like Eileen has.

HABITS OF SUCCESS

Step 1: Facing the Reality

Eileen took a brave step by confronting her financial situation head-on. She meticulously documented her income, expenses, and outstanding debts. This raw confrontation with reality was both daunting and liberating. It marked the beginning of her journey towards financial empowerment.

Step 2: Seeking Knowledge

Recognizing the importance of financial literacy, Eileen dove into books, online courses, and workshops. She absorbed knowledge about budgeting, saving, and investing. Eileen's newfound understanding allowed her to make informed decisions, turning her financial ignorance into empowerment.

With this knowledge, Eileen, as you may have guessed by now is this author, created her Credit Education Business, *Credit Knowhow, LLC* and now empowers many women entrepreneurs through her expertise.

Let's continue with Eileen's transformation.

Step 3: Building a Support System

Realizing the strength in community, Eileen sought advice from financial experts and joined support groups. She learned from others who had faced similar challenges and triumphed. This support system not only provided practical insights but also emotional encouragement, reinforcing her resilience.

As Eileen worked with her Mentors, people and opportunities that she never imagined began to appear, as if out of nowhere.

Step 4: Budgeting Mastery

Armed with knowledge and support, Eileen crafted a comprehensive Cash Flow Prosperity Plan. She identified areas where she could cut unnecessary expenses and reallocated funds towards debt repayment and savings. The discipline she instilled in budgeting became the foundation for her financial recovery.

Step 5: Embracing Side Ventures

To augment her income, Eileen explored side ventures aligned with her skills and passions. She freelanced in educating others on credit basics, credit scoring and cash flow planning, turning her creative talents into a lucrative source of additional income. This not only eased her financial burden but also ignited a sense of entrepreneurial spirit.

Step 6: Goal Setting

Eileen set clear financial goals for herself and her business. Whether it was creating an emergency fund, saving for her business education, or achieving homeownership, these goals provided direction and motivation. Eileen's determination to secure a better future for herself fueled her commitment to financial success.

Step 7: Celebrating Small Wins

In the midst of her financial journey, Eileen learned the importance of celebrating small victories. Each debt paid off, every financial milestone reached—she acknowledged these achievements, fostering a positive mindset. This celebration of small wins fueled her perseverance through challenges.

As time passed, her dedication bore fruit. Her debt diminished, savings grew, and the dreams she once thought unattainable started to materialize. She transformed from a woman grappling with financial woes to a beacon of inspiration for others facing similar struggles. Her journey illuminated the path towards financial empowerment, proving that with resilience, knowledge, and support, anyone can overcome the toughest financial situation.

HABITS OF SUCCESS

Know your Numbers

Here is a 5-step process to understand and manage the financial aspects of your business:

Organize Financial Records:

Start by organizing and maintaining accurate financial records. This includes income statements, balance sheets, and cash flow statements. Utilize accounting software or hire a professional accountant to ensure all transactions are recorded systematically. Well-organized financial records serve as the foundation for informed decision-making.

Budgeting and Forecasting: Cash Flow Prosperity Plan

Develop a detailed budget that outlines both income and expenses. Break down fixed and variable costs to understand where money is being allocated. Additionally, create financial forecasts to estimate future revenues and expenditures. Regularly compare actual financial performance against the budget and forecast to identify any deviations and make necessary adjustments.

Financial Ratios and Analysis:

Utilize financial ratios and analysis to assess the health and performance of the business. Key ratios include profitability ratios, liquidity ratios, and efficiency ratios. Analyzing these metrics provides insights into the business's financial strengths and areas that may require attention. It's a crucial step in making strategic decisions to optimize financial performance.

Cash Flow Management:

Pay close attention to cash flow, as it is the lifeblood of any business. Create cash flow forecasts to anticipate periods of surplus or shortfall. Implement strategies to optimize cash flow, such as negotiating favorable payment terms with suppliers or encouraging prompt customer payments. Effective cash flow management ensures the business can meet its financial obligations and seize opportunities for growth.

Regular Financial Reviews:

Conduct regular financial reviews to stay proactive and informed. Set aside dedicated time to assess financial reports, review key performance indicators, and evaluate the overall financial health of the business. Regular reviews empower the entrepreneur to make data-driven decisions, identify trends, and pivot strategies if needed.

By following this 5-step process, a woman entrepreneur can gain a thorough understanding of the financial landscape of her business. This knowledge not only facilitates day-to-day operations but also empowers her to make strategic decisions that contribute to the long-term success and sustainability of the business.

As a Financial Architect for business owners, I am thrilled when my clients have that "aha" moment when we are working together on their Cash Flow Prosperity Plan. We dive in deep and create their Revenue Model and their Credit Analysis and they come away empowered and impassioned to continue to grow their business.

Follow along with these steps and just like Eileen (yes, it's me), your opportunities will expand, your circle of friendship will explode with the right people, and your confidence in yourself and your business will flourish.

Be your best self—you owe it to You!

EILEEN E. GALBRAITH

About Eileen E Galbraith: As a Financial Architect for Business, entrepreneurs hire Eileen to build their influence and scale their profits because most lack essential methods and channels to create success, lack funding opportunities, and may face continuous struggles resulting in business disarray. So, Eileen helps them define, align, and design a visible, credible, and sustaining business. Financial disarray is a precursor to failure—do not let that happen to your business!

Eileen is a Compassionate Kick-ass Coach. She can kick your butt in financial shape and make things happen, but she's also very compassionate. She knows what people need, what they want, and how to deliver it.

Eileen is a Certified FICO Pro, an International Best-Selling Author and Speaker, a sought-after Business Success Coach, and the Founder of Renewed Abundance and Credit Knowhow. She has run multi-million-dollar businesses throughout her career and increased cash flow and profitability throughout her markets. Recognized as a professional Business Coach, Eileen positions her clients toward optimal possibilities, such as optimizing their personal credit to position themselves to build credit in the name of their business. This all-important step opens the doors to Financial Creditability, Fundability, and Business Growth. Eileen has a high-energy, no-nonsense approach and loves supporting people with their goals. Just look for the Dancing Queen, and you will find Eileen!

Author's Website: www.CreditKnowHow.biz

Book Series Website: www.ThePrinciplesOfDebbieAndGoliath.com

THE PRINCIPLES OF DEBBIE & GOLIATH

HABITS OF SUCCESS

THE PRINCIPLES OF DEBBIE & GOLIATH

> Women are always saying, 'We can do anything men can do.' But men should be saying, 'We can do anything that women can do.'
>
> ~ Gloria Steinem

HABITS OF SUCCESS

ELIZABETH ANNE WALKER
THE POWER OF READING & PERSONAL DEVELOPMENT

There is a modern movement called baby-led growth. This is where the parents of a young child allow the child to develop at their own pace with minimal intervention until the child is ready. For example, not sitting the child up until the child does it themselves, not propping the child into the crawling position, and not reading to a child until they express an interest in books. This is indeed an interesting movement and is vastly different from what both I received as a child and the way I parented my own children.

Reading was very important in my family, and I recall being read to at a very young age. I, myself, as a parent read to my children from the day they were born. In their little hospital cots, we did reading time. Why? Because the vast knowledge and believe it or not worldly experience I had gained from being read to and reading books was so valuable to me I wanted to impress that upon my children. I wanted their brains to grow and develop in the way mine had. I wanted them to have the best opportunities in life and to me that all started with the ability to read.

As a child, we had a family book that came out every Christmas. It was called *Santa's Workshop*. I still have it and I am excited to read it to my grandchild who is due in a few months. This book smelled old, it had a few colour plate illustrations and large writing so as a child I could read along. As the eldest grandchild, years later I would read it to my nephews and niece. The joy and wonder in this one book led to a love and curiosity of just what might be on the pages of every other book I have ever read.

The development of a person is vast and convoluted and is steeped in tradition both societal and familial. And it is not until we are of an adult nature, let's say somewhere between 15 and 20 that we realise the value of our own development. The problem is at this point our challenges may have already been created and may be as big as Goliath in nature. So, we start down the personal development route and "try" to learn as much as we can. It often starts with books and if you've never read before (accepting what you were forced to read in school) then here is challenge number one!

No need to worry, you can get an audiobook. Have you ever wondered what the difference between an audiobook and reading is? It's the development of the characters and scene using your own voice in your head, your own memories, and your own ideas that is the difference. When you listen to an audiobook with someone else's voice you tend to create imagery in your mind that you assume someone with that voice would create, as opposed to that which you would naturally create. Rather than a major problem, it's just a minor limitation.

And it's ok you will gain some value as your brain continues to personally develop. Or will you? You see if the love of books is not created as a child, statistics say you are less likely to enjoy any kind of reading whether it is traditional or audio. And the irony of this is I am here writing this information in a book!

So, where are we at…. You can avoid your Goliath if you learn to read? If your mum or dad valued reading you will too? That if you read you automatically personally develop. That's what I thought too!

There is another pathway to personal development though, one that we often pretend does not exist and one that we rarely celebrate. It is the path of ongoing Goliaths. The path of continuous hard knocks and challenges, the path of adversity. The path my son took. He hated reading, he refused to read, and I doubt now that he is 23 that he has ever read a book since he was 5 or 6 years old. Personal development though is far from foreign to him, it wasn't always this way.

14 years old living in Sydney Australia, living with mum half the time and dad half the time, angry at the world because his parents couldn't love him enough to stay together. Gets into the wrong crowd and starts using drugs. Mum from an upper-middle-class old-fashioned values family has no idea what to do except blame herself for being a terrible mum. Dad from a working-class family joins in. While I destroy myself with guilt ("maybe I should have accepted the abuse to keep the family together") my son destroys himself with substances.

Well, I read and read and read and read. Everything I could find on parenting, teenage drug use, etc., etc., and nothing made sense or helped me to feel any better. He partied, and partied, and partied, and partied, and nothing he did made him feel any better. My hair fell out and I became incredibly unwell. He lost weight dramatically and became incredibly unwell. There was nothing I could do for him, by now he barely answered a text let alone a call and he hadn't slept a night at home in about a year.

I had to do the one thing the books said that I hadn't done, I had to start living for me. Personal development became an integral part of my life, I did the courses, I read the books, I went to seminars and trainings, and little by little as I got better and learned to love myself more, so did he! The more I invested in me the more I was able to help him without actually even speaking to him.

Fast forward to now. I run one of the biggest personal development businesses in Australia, my son works for me as our Nurture manager and spends most of his time helping mummas who have lost their sons to drugs or other distractions. Every single time, as the mumma evolves so does the son. I am so grateful for the gift of reading I had, my gateway to personal development. I am so grateful for the experiences my son had, and his gateway to personal development. I am so grateful that we work together to make a large impact on the world and help others find their gateways to a happy and fulfilling life.

P.S. He got married a little while ago and now we are expecting his son and my first grandbaby in March 2024.

ELIZABETH ANNE WALKER

About Elizabeth Anne Walker: Elizabeth is Australia's leading Female Integrated NLP Trainer, an international speaker with Real Success, and the host of Success Resources's (Australia's largest and most successful events promoter, including speakers such as Tony Robbins and Sir Richard Branson) inaugural Australian Women's Program "The Seed." Elizabeth has guided many people to achieve complete personal breakthroughs and phenomenal personal and business growth. With over 25 years of experience transforming the lives of hundreds of thousands of people, Elizabeth's goal is to assist leaders to create the reality they choose to live, impacting millions on a global scale.

A thought leader who has worked alongside people like Gary Vaynerchuck, Kerwin Rae, Jeffery Slayter, and Kate Gray, Elizabeth has an outstanding method of delivering heart with business.

As a former lecturer in medicine at the University of Sydney and lecturer in nursing at Western Sydney University, Elizabeth was instrumental in the research and development of the stillbirth and neonatal death pathways, ensuring each family in Australia went home knowing what happened to their child, and felt understood, heard, and seen.

A former Australian Champion in Trampolining and Australian Dance sport, Elizabeth has always been passionate about the mindset and skills required to create the results you are seeking.

Author's Website: www.ElizabethAnneWalker.com

Book Series Website: www.ThePrinciplesOfDebbieAndGoliath.com

HABITS OF SUCCESS

FATIMA HURD
BREAKING FREE

As a child, I always dreamed of having enough money to never worry about not having any. Growing up, all I heard was money doesn't grow on trees. You need to work hard to earn a good living. My parents modeled decent money-management skills. However, all my life, most women in our family felt they had to depend on their spouse to have a comfortable life, which worked in those times. Or at least they made it work. But that came at a price for the women in the family.

Even though my mom was the one who managed the finances in our home, she still didn't feel confident enough to be out on her own, so she stayed in a marriage that was toxic and was not the best situation for many years before finally owning her confidence and breaking free from the limiting belief that she was unable to "make it" on her own.

When I was 16, my mom finally had enough and ended her marriage. I was in awe of how quickly and easily she got on her feet. She rented her first very own apartment without anyone to help her, she was promoted at work, and things began to fall into place for us. I was so proud of her. Her story inspired me and made me realize that we truly are responsible for our choices and our happiness! I've never seen my mom more at peace and as happy as that day when we were moving into our little apartment. That apartment was tiny compared to the home we left behind, but it was all worth it! We lived in peace and joy. I will never forget the sense of freedom and joy I experienced for the first time in my life in that moment!

HABITS OF SUCCESS

I was too young to understand that that moment would have a powerful impact on my life one day. Seeing my mom thrive independently made me realize we are responsible for our destiny. My mom's F.E.A.R (false evidence appearing real) of losing everything and ending up on the streets is what kept her a prisoner of her own limiting belief. Her grade school education, three kids, and limited English validated in her mind that she was indeed going to fail even if she tried, so she didn't until the pain became unbearable. She knew she needed to get out.

Why do we wait until the pain becomes so intense to take action? Fast forward: those same fears became my fears as a grown-up. Having three children of my own, I feared failing as a mom, wife, and provider. And unlike my mom, these fears had no validation. I always excelled at any job I had. I always wanted to do more, be the best version of myself, and create a better life for my family than the one I had. But no one teaches those things—at least, I didn't have a mentor until I was in my early 20's.

Creating habits and structure helped my mom break the limiting beliefs that kept her stuck. Healthy habits helped my mom achieve financial freedom and break her from the limiting beliefs that kept her stuck in the false reality that she could never be-do-have unless she had someone else in her life to depend on. The fear that she was not smart enough, or not deserving enough, or just not enough to be successful was instilled in her all throughout her childhood, and then as an adult in her marriage. She finally picked up some books that helped her shift her mindset and put on the path to help herself and us.

Even though my situation was different from hers, like my dad, my husband has always been supportive regarding my finances. He is a family man, and he has always made it a priority to make sure he takes care of his family. However, it took me a while to understand that my own limiting beliefs around money were keeping "US" broke—my fear was taking away from our family! It didn't matter how much money came in; we were always barely making it. And it was my own belief of not being good enough that kept us in scarcity. My thoughts and my experiences from childhood gave me a false perceptive that we were broke even when we weren't.

THE PRINCIPLES OF DEBBIE & GOLIATH

This scarcity mentality showed up in my journey as an entrepreneur. When I first started my journey in entrepreneurship, I had a business partner. She was great at marketing, and she did all of our marketing. When things didn't work out, and I was on my own, I partnered with someone else. There was always this fear that I couldn't do this without someone else who had more experience than I, and unfortunately, the business would fail every time I partnered with someone.

When I made the decision to finally be on my own and run my business without a partner, there was a lot of failing forward and a low start. But when I finally acknowledged the fact that I had to face my fears and my finances and create a structure to finally set myself free from scarcity, I began to thrive. Success was in facing the fear of failing, and when I began to work toward conquering the Goliath (doubt, taking action, self-sabotaging), I focused on what I wanted by creating awareness and taking action in doing things differently that actually moved the needle forward for my business. I realized that the one thing stopping me from finding success was the fear of not making money because that is where my focus was.

So, I shifted my mindset to asking empowering questions, owning my finances by looking at them and knowing where my money was going, and lastly, keeping myself accountable shifted me towards the direction of creating instead of lacking. The following are steps I followed to help through the process of breaking through my limiting belief around financial codependency.

Breaking free from financial codependency can be challenging, but it's an important step toward personal independence and financial stability. Here are some steps to help:

1. Self-awareness and Acknowledgment

- Recognize the Patterns: Acknowledge the behaviors and dependencies that contribute to financial codependency.
- Understand Triggers: Identify the situations or emotions that lead to codependent financial behaviors.

HABITS OF SUCCESS

2. Education and Understanding

- Financial Literacy: Invest time in learning about personal finance, budgeting, investing, and debt management. This knowledge empowers you to make informed decisions.
- Seek Support: Consider workshops, courses, or financial counseling to gain practical skills and guidance.

3. Set Boundaries and Establish Independence

- Define Personal Boundaries: Clearly define what financial boundaries are acceptable and necessary for your well-being.
- Develop Financial Independence: Gradually reduce financial interdependence by working toward financial autonomy. This could involve opening your own bank accounts, building your credit, or finding ways to earn your income.

4. Create a Realistic Budget and Financial Plan

- Track Expenses: Monitor your spending habits to understand where your money goes.
- Set Financial Goals: Create short-term and long-term financial goals that align with your values and aspirations.
- Budgeting: Develop a realistic budget that allows you to save, invest, and cover essential expenses while limiting unnecessary spending.

5. Communicate and Seek Support

- Open Dialogue: Discuss your intentions and plans with those involved in your finances, communicating your goals and boundaries clearly.
- Therapy or Support Groups: Consider therapy or support groups focused on codependency to address underlying emotional aspects of financial dependency.

6. Practice Self-Care and Mindfulness

- Emotional Well-being: Prioritize self-care activities and practices that support emotional well-being, reducing stress and anxiety around finances.
- Mindfulness: Practice mindfulness techniques to stay present and make conscious financial decisions rather than reactive ones.

7. Take Action and Stay Consistent

- Implement Changes Gradually: Break free from financial codependency gradually, implementing changes step by step.
- Stay Consistent: Consistency in following your budget, boundaries, and financial plan is key to breaking free from old patterns.

8. Evaluate and Adjust

- Regular Reviews: Periodically assess your financial progress, reassess goals, and make adjustments to your plan as needed.
- Learn from Setbacks: Embrace setbacks as learning opportunities and adjust strategies accordingly.

9. Celebrate Milestones

- Acknowledge Achievements: Celebrate your milestones and successes, no matter how small. It reinforces positive financial habits and motivates further progress.

Breaking free from financial codependency is a process that takes time, patience, and consistent effort.

HABITS OF SUCCESS

Special Dedication to Arabella Hurd:

"The path to success is to take massive, determined action."
"Setting goals is the first step in turning the invisible into the visible."
"Goals are like magnets. They'll attract the things that make them come true."
"One reason so few of us achieve what we truly want is that we never direct our focus; we never concentrate our power."
"Successful people ask better questions, and as a result, they get better answers."

Never value your worth based on someone else's efforts! Be your own boss, baby girl; you've got this!

~ Mom

FATIMA HURD

About Fatima Hurd: In addition to her professional achievements, Fatima Hurd is also a talented photographer who has a passion for working with and photographing female entrepreneurs. She believes in the power of visual storytelling and understands the importance of showcasing authenticity in front of the camera. Fatima's photography sessions with female entrepreneurs are not just about capturing beautiful images, but also about empowering them to show up authentically. She creates a safe and supportive environment where her clients can feel comfortable being themselves and expressing their unique personalities and stories. Through her photography, Fatima aims to capture the essence and spirit of each individual she works with. She believes that by showcasing the authentic selves of female entrepreneurs, she can help them build a strong personal brand and connect with their target audience on a deeper level.

Fatima's diverse skill set as an OBA Coach, certified hypnotherapist, Best-Selling Author, and photographer allows her to provide a holistic approach to empowering and supporting female entrepreneurs. She understands the challenges they face in both their personal and professional lives and is dedicated to helping them overcome obstacles and achieve their goals. With her passion for helping others and her commitment to making a positive impact in the world, Fatima Hurd is not only a successful professional but also a role model for women who aspire to live authentically and make a difference in their own lives and the lives of others.

Author's Website: *www.FatimaHurd.com*

Book Series Website: *www.ThePrinciplesOfDebbieAndGoliath.com*

HABITS OF SUCCESS

JOANNA JAMES
MY DARLING SELF

As you enter the 13th year around the sun, you will start to see that your world is changing. As you enter a time between being a child and an adult, you will naturally seek to define yourself within this world. Don't be fooled by the short-term view of things as people in life try to influence you, knowing who you are is a lifetime journey. At times, there will be pressure placed upon you to change or conform to others' expectations. When you find yourself amidst this, always remember that the only person you ultimately need to answer to is yourself.

Amongst all of life's events, you will have people share their wisdom; the key is recognizing what is useful, when to listen and, more importantly, to act upon it. As you experiment here, you will make lots of mistakes so see these stumbling blocks for what they are, merely milestones and opportunities to learn upon the journey. No matter what age or situation you find yourself in, remember that the most important thing to do is to love yourself completely and that at any moment in time you can be anyone you choose to be.

Everything in life is based on the choices you make, even when you abstain or are indecisive you are making a choice in that moment to avoid a decision. We create our lives in every aspect, both the good and the bad. We are 24/7 imagination machines creating our day-to-day reality. The quicker you can learn to master your mind, the better things will be, and the more you will be able to master your own destiny. The trick is not to get distracted with all the myriad of people and events that occur in between.

HABITS OF SUCCESS

Begin to think of yourself as a walking antenna sending and receiving signals constantly. This world is ruled by 12 laws that are often not explained clearly so it is your mission to find and understand them. Just like an apple falls from a tree due to gravity, this world operates energetically based on a series of rules that are unseen. I wish I had had someone explain them to me as I grew into a woman as it surely would have helped me navigate life more elegantly.

1. Everything and everyone in life are connected. We are but different fractals of the same being. What we do to each other we in fact share collectively, even if in the moment it does not present that way. Few people see this clearly and so live out life feeling separate from the rest of humanity.

2. Everything in life vibrates and is in motion with a unique energy signature. There will never be anyone exactly the same as you. Embrace your uniqueness; it is the gift of life. Relish and expand upon it at every opportunity.

3. Life is a series of repeating patterns. As you grow in age, you will see this occur regularly the same story or type of event repeating again and again. When you encounter events that you do not understand, look for the patterns in them. Some may occur quickly in a matter of days and others may take years on the stage. When you understand this principle, you will be able to create changes to the manuscript of the play.

4. Become the kind of person you want to be in this world—for like attracts like. Consciously decide what you want to experience and choose to be a living demonstration of it. This is the quickest way to guarantee you will experience it. If you want love, be loving. If you want to be treated with kindness, be kind to yourself.

5. Everything and I mean everything requires action. Thinking about things will not bring results alone; you must implement things, regularly and swiftly. All life starts with a thought and an idea, but it is a requirement to place that seed into action in order to create what you want.

6. The only thing in life that is guaranteed is change. Learn to run with it, roll with what life presents you, be adaptable, let go of the old and embrace the change in front of you. Life is merely a journey where you are changing form regularly. No one escapes it. The more fluid you become the easier the transitions will be for change will be both planned and unexpected.

7. Everything you do will return to you. Every good deed, every dark thought, and every action will have an equal and opposite reaction so choose your thoughts, words, and actions wisely. It may or may not return immediately, it may take many years, and it may return in a slightly different package, but it is 100% guaranteed it will visit you in some way.

8. You will receive what you give, so give generously of your time, your love your passions, the fastest way to get anything is to give it first. Unbelievable but true, just try it and you will soon see that it is absolutely true.

9. Nothing in life is either good or bad without comparing it to another. Remember with all that you do everything is relative so be sure to always put things into perspective.

10. Everything has an equal opposite, don't expect things to all be the same or right or perfect, life is made up of duality and it will often swing in between things. Most importantly should you find yourself in more difficult times, remember it's all in preparation to swing to the upside of life so maintain a positive attitude.

11. Everything happens in cycles. Some are short like the minutes in an hour, others take a year like the seasons and some take decades or even centuries to move through. Life is a series of cycles which will place varying degrees of influence on you so accept that and it will make the journey easier particularly as you age.

12. Everything is both yin and yang. Regardless of your gender at birth, you will have both masculine and feminine energies within you; learn to embrace them and use them as you choose to, for like everything else they are proportional to how you choose to express them.

HABITS OF SUCCESS

So, whilst life is always happening on a higher level beyond our comprehension, you are a human being experiencing things in a physical way. So, when the drama of life unfolds and the universal laws temporarily escape you, the following list of 13 principles will help to guide you when decisions are to be made.

- The only person who can discover the truth of your life is you; it's a journey you start and finish alone so take time to reflect for yourself along the way.

- You have 2 ears and 1 mouth so it's always best to listen more than you speak.

- It's not what people say that matters, it's what they do that's important. When unsure of a person's intentions, always watch if their actions match what they say, and you will quickly determine if they are genuine. Extend respect and trust easily, and withdraw it quickly if someone seeks advantage by gaining power over you.

- Never mistake kindness for weakness—it's often much more challenging to do what's the right thing to do. This is where a person's character is made, and your character will define the storybook of the life you write.

- Look after your body—it is your vessel for life, and you will need it for a long time, so eat well, stay fit, and drink lots of clean water. A short-term fix can create long-term complications. Avoid environmental toxins, this planet is full of harmful chemicals disguised in the products we eat, wear, and use in the places we live in.

- Try not to judge others for you will never truly know the internal reality that person is living. In turn, do not take on the judgment others hold over you as it is simply none of their business anyway. Practicing both of these things will give you great freedom. Remember the meaning you make that will determine your experience of things.

- Regret is always best avoided so take time to think about the longer term when making decisions, even if that is only just a few hours ahead.

THE PRINCIPLES OF DEBBIE & GOLIATH

- When deep emotions come to you, know they are just intense bursts of energy in motion (e-motion). Allow them to move through you and feel them to their very depths. Expressing them is a central part of life. It's when you hold onto things that you may fall prey to becoming stuck. It's here we can create pain that lingers for years. Forgiveness is a wonderful practice as it will set you free; it is never about the person you are releasing, although they too will feel it (Universal Law # 1).

- There is nothing to fear in life other than fear itself, learn to look it in the eye and be calm, as all fear is simply an illusion of the mind. It's what you believe in the moment that is most important here.

- To master your mind, listen to what you are really telling yourself on the inside because that is where you truly create from. Dedicate daily practice to instructing your mind on how you want the program to run. Even if it's not your current reality, your mind is malleable to what you tell it to be true, so use this practice to your advantage every day with everything that you do.

- You are always guided, there are always benevolent people and beings that love and adore, so know that you are never alone, and help is always on the way.

- Joy is one of the highest vibrational states in life so be sure to follow your heart and dedicate practice to experiencing it daily.

- Should you find yourself in any type of despair, remember that hope is the highest potential of all, it conquers all darkness so maintain your focus upon it.

My dearest self, I am so proud of the person you are. You are a beautiful soul with a special purpose for being here at this time. Trust the lessons that will guide your way and light your path. You are important, your life here is important, and, most importantly, know I love you no matter what happens along the way. Shine bright, be brave, live life fearlessly for to be alive is a gift every day. Remember to relish every step along the way. It is cliche, but there will come a time when you will say, "Goodness, the time passed quickly."

HABITS OF SUCCESS

Time is the most valuable resource you will ever have, so learn to use it wisely.

JOANNA JAMES

About Joanna James: Joanna James is known as a revolutionary difference maker in the Design, Construction, and Banking sectors and is featured in publications such as Entrepreneur, USA Today, The Advisor, MPA, Australian Broker, Flaunt, CIO, and Insights Success.

As Australia's youngest registered female architect and builder, she is known as creator of the world's first 'Bio' home, featured on TV series 'I Own Australia's Best Home.'

Joanna created the Shambhala@byron retreat which welcomed celebrity singer Sting as her first guest. Her book Mind Body Spaces raises awareness around our health and the spaces that we live in. A pioneering entrepreneur for the Mortgage Ezy Group of companies, her contribution shines through the 32 Industry awards including 3 times BRW fastest company.

A passionate advocate for women in business, Joanna has also been recognized as Principal of the Year (WIFA), Top 100 Female Entrepreneurs, and Top 100 Female Mentors. Contributing to the FBAA Artemis Forum, she works to raise opportunities for Education, Advocacy, and Awareness for women within the Australian Finance Industry.

Author's Website: *www.JoannaJames.com*

Book Series Website: *www.ThePrinciplesOfDebbieAndGoliath.com*

HABITS OF SUCCESS

KATHERINE VARGAS
AMAZING GRACE

"Little girl, I say to you, get up!"
~ **Mark 5:41**

My name is Katherine, and I am one of God's chosen surrogate mothers. What does that mean? That means I am a mother to three beautiful children, but only one living child.

When I was seventeen years old, I saw my niece being born. My mother lied and told the hospital I was eighteen so I could stay in the room while my older sister was in labor. I saw the natural birth of my niece and from then on, I vowed I would not have children; that was too traumatizing. Fast forward about thirteen years later, and all I wanted was to become a mother.

I went the traditional route, met a man, fell in love, was married two years later, had a big wedding. We bought a condo and waited a few months to have a child. I am Mexican, so I thought it would be incredibly easy to get pregnant. I was wrong. After about a year of trial and error, $500+ of acupuncture, and after a complete surrender to God, I was finally pregnant.

I had already dreamed that I would have my little girl Marina, named after my best friend, my grandma Marina. Marina is my perfect little peanut. Small but mighty in every way. I refer to her as my "spicy peanut" due to her sassiness and small stature. God gave me the perfect gift in 2018—He gave me her.

HABITS OF SUCCESS

January 2020 arrived; strange things were happening in the world. Although there was so much uncertainty, my husband and I decided to take a risk, sell our condo, and move to our "Dream city," the one we really wanted to raise a family in but was nowhere in reach for us financially.

Fortunately, my Godfather helped us find the cheapest home in the nicest neighborhood. Everything was looking up when the world was falling apart. We bought our house and began turning it into our home: we loved our neighbors, I was back in school to obtain my Master's, and I was ready to start a side gig as a mobile Notary for extra income. In my mind, 2021 was looking prosperous for us!

October of 2020, we learned I was pregnant. I thought, "What a perfect age gap for Marina and her future sibling." We were thrilled. I just had to keep it a secret a little longer. December 2020, I went to my appointment ready to hear the heartbeat. Unfortunately, I didn't.

I was 9 weeks pregnant, and the doctors somehow estimated I miscarried at around 7 weeks. I tried to pass the baby naturally, but the baby did not want to leave my body. If I waited any longer, I would risk my own life.

After a few days, the doctor finally ordered me to go to the ER. The male doctor handed me two pills. One to take at the hospital and one to take home. He told me I would experience some "light cramping" and it would be over.

I took the pill, went home, and within a few hours I was crying in the fetal position experiencing the worst physical and psychological pain I had ever experienced in my life. My husband told my daughter I was sick, and he tried to put her to bed so I could pass our child in the bathroom without her knowing. I just remember laying in the shower, crying for what seemed like forever, exhausted, and defeated. Eventually, it was over. My little Ruby was gone.

I sat in grief for weeks. The holidays were so hard to enjoy with fears of Covid and trying not to have an emotional breakdown in front of my family. I dropped out of school, stopped my notary training, and just grieved. I didn't have the motivation anymore. I didn't have the same goals I had just two months prior. My fire was out.

At the same time, I had my daughter Marina. She was in this very fun age. She was so inquisitive, so in tune with my emotions and feelings. She still needed mommy and mommy needed to get it together. I remember at one point reading this story in the Bible about how this little girl's parents went to Jesus and begged Him to heal her. She was dead. Jesus went to the girl's lifeless body, took her hand, and said "Talithia koum!" which means, "Little girl, I say to you, get up!"

When I read that, I felt it so deep in my soul. I felt like I was that little lifeless girl, and He was telling me, get up! I'm here now, you're fine, get up, little girl. So, I did. Although the pandemic was not fully over, I told my husband I needed to go back to church in person. I needed to heal from this pain. We began attending in person church, I joined one of the group studies, and I began therapy.

Within a few months, I shifted my focus on health and healing rather than education and career planning. I started becoming vulnerable. I started asking for help. Although I did "get up", I wasn't strong just yet but knew I could get there again. I began to eat better and exercise. I gained energy and strength. I needed it, especially when I found out my niece was pregnant, and her due date was my Ruby's due date (in July). I felt like God was telling me she needed me now the way I needed her when my daughter was born. It was a painful request, but I was so excited over this new blessing.

A few weeks later, I found out I was pregnant again. I attribute that pregnancy to my "health journey." I was in this women's fitness group called 'Grit and Grace' so I thought it would be cute, if I was pregnant with a girl, to name her Grace. Due to my age at this point, and the fact that I had a miscarriage a few months earlier, I had to see a high-risk specialist.

I was so impatient; I went without my husband to that appointment. The ultrasound tech came in, she showed me the baby and then the best part... I heard the heartbeat! Nice and loud. I had these thick warm tears streaming down my face and over my smile. I could not contain my excitement and relief anymore; that heartbeat was music to my ears. The ultrasound tech gave me a tissue, told me to sit tight until the doctor can review the images and advised me he would be in shortly. I laid back in pure bliss, thanking God profusely.

The doctor came in, introduced himself, and let me know he reviewed the ultrasound. He put the images on a screen for me and pointed at the back of the baby's head and said, "This is my concern." Once he said those words, I went into complete shock and panic. Everything he said after I needed him to repeat because I couldn't process anything he was trying to explain to me. I told him I just had a miscarriage, and I couldn't take anymore bad news. He explained that there was too much fluid behind the baby's neck and that I could undergo genetic testing. He would set up a meeting with a genetic counselor for more information.

I went to my car and cried hot tears of anger. I called my husband and could hardly speak. He later told me that when I called him, he thought the baby was dead already, just from the way I was crying. He hung up and headed home immediately. I called my best friend, Teresa, who had a very similar story in 2015: she made the decision to terminate her pregnancy after multiple appointments of only bad news. She was the first person to tell me, "Do not abort the baby, you will regret it, you can do this."

I hung up with her and called my mother. I could hardly breathe, but I had to get to the lab to begin these tests so I drove to the lab while my mother told me, "God won't give you what you can't handle." Again, it was nothing I wanted to hear. I could not fathom losing another child; I felt like I was being punished for something. I went to the lab, had my first of many blood draws, and went home to cry.

The next day, we met with the genetic counselor; we answered a series of questions about both sides of our family medical history. No one on either side had genetic disorders. She then went through the possibilities of which genetic disorder we were looking at, but they were all under the "Trisomy" umbrella which meant the baby had three copies of chromosomes instead of two.

THE PRINCIPLES OF DEBBIE & GOLIATH

After weeks of testing and waiting extra weeks for results, we were mentally and emotionally battling over what was the best course of action, all the while my baby was growing inside of me. On the final decision day, I asked if I could see her one more time on the ultrasound before we made our decision. The doctor, who at this point was frustrated that we wouldn't just terminate her, left the room. The ultrasound tech turned on the machine and we saw her, and this little girl waved at us. She waved, like she was asking for our mercy and strength. We decided to keep her, the doctor referred us elsewhere to continue treatment (I guess we were no longer worth his time), and we prepared to have a child with Trisomy 18, a fetal fatal diagnosis.

Here is the long story short: we had an army of support around us because, through therapy, we learned to be vulnerable and ask for help and seek help. We prepared our daughter Marina as much as possible; we told her that she was a big sister—however, her little sister was chosen by God to be a princess in the kingdom of heaven.

I wanted to announce my pregnancy (because everyone could eventually tell I was pregnant) and I wanted to explain what was next. I posted about her on social media, letting everyone know, yes, I was pregnant, however due to her fetal fatal diagnosis we were not bringing her home. Instead, I encouraged everyone to send a gift to a local pregnancy center in Huntington Beach under the name "Grace Vargas" in her honor. This pregnancy center received about 60 packages in about one month from that post. The pregnancy center thanked us by bringing us in as a family to introduce Marina to her little sister via 4D Ultrasound.

I joined a Trisomy 18 support group on Facebook. I made friends with other trisomy moms, both through that group and through other mutual friends. The hard truth was hitting us hard as we realized that her odds were against us. Our friends had their baby in November, and she died 9 days later. We were due in December. The week she was due, I was a mess. We changed her birth plan to be a scheduled c-section so it would be less stressful on her body. December 9th was Marina's Christmas recital at school. We watched her nervously on stage. We ate dinner as a family, and we sent her off with my mother-in-law for the night.

December 10th, very early in the morning, we headed to the hospital. The staff at the new hospital treated us like VIP from the minute we were referred to them (we still keep in touch with our fetal care coordinator). They had her birth plan; they knew she would not see the NICU but only be in our arms the entire time. We had the C-section not knowing if she would live through it, but then we heard this miraculous little sound of a kitten, and that kitten was our three-pound miracle baby girl, Grace.

Our family and friends flooded our room over the next four days: Marina got to meet her sister, we had photos, prayers, and lots of hope! I remember just holding her, begging God to let me keep her. The doctors and nurses in general labor and delivery loved checking her because they were only used to seeing babies that small in the NICU. She was thriving on her own.

They sent us home after four days. Our family and church had quickly gathered micro-preemie items for us to take her home. The reality was, we were also going home with a triage team. The reality was, she still had trisomy. We tried to enjoy our time with her, anyway. Marina was a proud big sister and we were so happy to have had decorated before we went to the hospital so the girls could truly experience Christmas together. Christmas came and went; we saw very few family members because we did not want to expose the girls to any virus during our time together. It was still the best Christmas our little family had ever had. We had gifts and food delivered to our door every day. We called our family through video chats.

I remember being on video chat with Grace and my cousin Ronald. He was battling cancer at the time, and he was such a huge support throughout my miscarriage and through Grace's journey. Introducing them to each other via chat will forever hold a special memory in my heart.

A few days later, on December 28th, we learned some of our family members had COVID. We made sure to stay home and still just enjoy our time. My mother did come to pick up Marina, who, at this point, needed a break from being home. My husband worked in the garage to prevent draft from entering the house. I sat on the couch with my sleepy Grace bundled on my chest.

My husband came in the house, and I asked him to hold Grace so I could make tea. The next thing I knew, he was in a panic, taking her temperature and asking me to call 911. She was dying in his arms. I think she was waiting for him specifically to take her final breath. She had already had time with her sister, she had her time with me, she was just waiting to say goodbye to her daddy. So, she did.

One would think that losing your child is the worst thing in the world l, and it is. I do not recommend it to anyone! However, through faith, work, community and internal healing... This little girl got back up. God chose me not only to be a surrogate mother, but to share Grace's journey and the goodness and eternal impact she made not only in my life, but the lives of others as well.

I am now a parent education advocate for Horizon Pregnancy Clinic, and my husband and I have sat with quite a few families who have gone through or are going through similar journeys. Marina processes death as something both beautiful and sad, which is a healthier way than I ever processed death as a child or adult. Through us, Grace's legacy will live on, and I will continue to be a mom of three with my one (spicy) living and loving child.

KATHERINE VARGAS

About Katherine Vargas: Katherine Vargas is a dedicated and experienced professional specializing in the field of notary and loan signing services. Based in Orange County, CA, Katherine has established herself as a reliable Mobile Notary and Loan Signing Agent, known for her meticulous attention to detail and commitment to delivering top-quality service. Beyond her notary expertise, she is also recognized as a skilled Small Business Networking & Marketing Coach, where she leverages her extensive knowledge to help small businesses thrive in competitive markets.

Her expertise extends to legal intake, showcasing her versatility and comprehensive understanding of the legal aspects intertwined with her professional endeavors.

Katherine's website, *www.MrsKatherineVargas.com*, serves as a gateway for clients to access her services and benefit from her vast experience. Her proficiency, combined with her dedication to client satisfaction, makes her an invaluable asset to anyone seeking expert notary services, loan signing assistance, and business marketing coaching.

Author's Website: *www.MrsKatherineVargas.com*

Book Series Website: *www.ThePrinciplesOfDebbieAndGoliath.com*

KATIE MARES

NAVIGATING CHALLENGES TO UNLEASH THE EMPOWERED WOMAN WITHIN

Dear amazing young souls,

Consider this a heartfelt conversation, a compass guiding the fiery passion within your hearts and souls.

Life, akin to a breathtaking adventure, unfolds with unforeseen twists and turns. In your expedition through its diverse landscapes, you'll undoubtedly confront obstacles that may appear insurmountable. I share this letter not from a pedestal of unblemished triumph but from the depths of a profound journey, navigating one of the most challenging valleys of my life.

Personally, I have weathered formidable storms, surviving various forms of domestic abuse. I possess every justification to succumb, to surrender, to harbor resentment, and to lose faith in humanity. However, I haven't. You see, while you may not control the hand you're dealt, you unequivocally determine how you play those cards.

HABITS OF SUCCESS

For me, embracing life's journey and standing in my power, knowing I can shape my own narrative, has been the lifeline keeping me afloat in the roughest of seas.

Life is an unpredictable odyssey, and obstacles are its natural terrain. Rather than fearing them, welcome these challenges as opportunities for growth. Acknowledge that setbacks are not roadblocks but turns that lead to new horizons.

In this shared exploration, let's delve into four actions that can empower you to navigate the cards life deals.

Action 1: Cultivate Resilience

Resilience is the armor shielding you during life's tempests. Embrace setbacks as lessons, not failures. Remember, setbacks are ephemeral, but your resilience is enduring. Cultivate the mindset that adversity is a teacher, equipping you with the tools to face even greater challenges on your path to success.

Trust Your Instincts

Your intuition, a potent guide aligned with your true north, is your compass in the fog. Listen to that inner voice—it knows the way. In moments of uncertainty, your instincts will illuminate the path forward. Trusting yourself empowers you to make decisions in harmony with your values, goals, and dreams.

Action 2: Develop Self-Trust

Building trust in yourself is a gradual metamorphosis. Start by acknowledging even the smallest achievements. Celebrate your victories; let them serve as tangible evidence of your capabilities. Trusting yourself means recognizing the inner wisdom that enables you to overcome challenges and attain your aspirations.

THE PRINCIPLES OF DEBBIE & GOLIATH

Seek Mentorship

No one thrives in solitude. Mentorship is a catalyst that can illuminate your path and expedite your growth. Identify individuals who inspire you, those who have walked similar journeys, and seek their guidance. A mentor provides invaluable insights, shares wisdom, and offers support during challenging times.

Action 3: Connect with Mentors

Initiate connections with women who have triumphed in areas that resonate with you. Attend networking events, immerse yourself in mentorship programs, and engage on professional platforms. These relationships not only provide guidance but also establish a supportive network understanding the unique challenges and triumphs of global empowerment.

Continuously Learn

In our ever-evolving world, continuous learning is the cornerstone of staying ahead. Embrace a mindset of curiosity and lifelong learning. Seek opportunities to expand your knowledge, whether through formal education, online courses, or experiential learning.

Action 4: Commit to Lifelong Learning

Pledge to invest in your education and personal development regularly. Stay curious, explore new subjects, and challenge your assumptions. The more you learn, the more adaptable and resourceful you become, equipping yourself to conquer any obstacle that comes your way.

Dear incredible souls, life's journey is not about avoiding obstacles; it's about navigating them with courage, grace, and resilience. Each challenge you face is a testament to your strength and an opportunity to shape the empowered woman you are becoming. Embrace the journey, trust yourself, celebrate diversity, seek guidance, and commit to lifelong learning. You possess the power to conquer any obstacle and emerge victorious on your path to global empowerment.

With love and boundless belief in your potential,

XO,

Katie

KATIE MARES

About Katie Mares: As a brand experience expert, Katie knows firsthand the challenges organizations encounter as they strive to design a sustainable and effective CX program tailored for the female consumer. Using her experiences as a Chief Inspiration Officer, building company infrastructure and designing customer experience programs, she is now a leading voice for positive, actionable change in the organizations with which she partners. Katie has a Master's degree in Adult Training and Development from Schulich School of Business and a Certified Training and Development Professional (CTDP) certification.

As a highly sought-after speaker, Katie has inspired audiences around the world to think differently about the female consumer, customer experience, and leadership. She has worked with globally recognized brands, including Honda, Celebrity Cruises, and Canada Post.

Katie lives in Toronto with her three children. When she is not traveling around the world consulting and speaking, she can be found on a yoga mat, in a shoe store, or snuggled on the couch eating homemade popcorn and watching a movie with her three little ones.

Author's Website: *www.KatieMares.com*

Book Series Website: *www.ThePrinciplesOfDebbieAndGoliath.com*

HABITS OF SUCCESS

THE PRINCIPLES OF DEBBIE & GOLIATH

> There's something so special about a woman who dominates in a man's world. It takes a certain grace, strength, intelligence, fearlessness, and the nerve to never take no for an answer.
>
> ~ Rihanna

HABITS OF SUCCESS

LAUREN COBB
EMOTIONAL INTELLIGENCE

....

As I've looked back at my teenage years and my experiences, one of the biggest things that helped me was being in control of my emotions. As a teenager, I did not fully understand it or how that worked. Looking back, I can see people in my life who were teaching me it but it was never classified as such.

What did that look like?

It looked like my Dad coming to my room to talk to me after my mom and I got into a disagreement. It looked like my Grandma taking me to run errands with her to get out of the house when my mom wasn't in the best of head spaces, and talking me through it. It looked my teacher seeing me skipping class and hanging out with people who weren't the best of influences and pulling me aside to offer some unsolicited advice.

Thankfully, I was raised to develop values, and because of those who have taken me under their wings and have helped me to make better choices throughout my life… now I get to do the same for others, including my own daughters, friends and extended family.

These amazing people in my life were able to help me understand why others said things that were hurtful and why others would want to sabotage someone's character when they had done nothing to them. Why getting into a close romantic relationship wasn't the best choice as a teenager. A big lesson for me was that I could not change others. Those are just to name a few.

Obviously, if you are reading this book, congratulations—you are way ahead of your peers!

HABITS OF SUCCESS

What are the steps we take to learn what emotional intelligence is and how do we implement it in life?

1. **Self-Awareness:** How does others' behaviors affect you? Are you easily annoyed or frustrated by others? Are you able to listen and hear someone out without immediately becoming defensive or upset? And to flip the question, are you able to contain your excitement and happiness and show it in a contained way? We've all been the person or seen someone who blurts out screaming or shouting with excitement when they hear something they resonate with.

These aren't always bad things but knowing your audience and surroundings will make all the difference. Emotions can be the hardest to learn to recognize and understand how they impact you, but don't stress—with a bit of internal reflection and practice, it is possible! Identifying the cause of the feelings you're feeling will give you a better idea of what can be done to resolve the issue. Learning to do so will gain better listening skills and communication skills—as well as gain critical thinking and problem solving skills. So now that we are slowing down to notice HOW we feel in different situations and conversations we move into the next step.

2. We are in charge of how we choose to react: In MOST cases, choosing to not react quickly is the best option. It isn't ALWAYS possible to delay your response but when possible and especially while practicing and learning how to execute these skills, it is usually the best choice. When we choose take a step back and think of where the other person's actions are coming from, we are able to think more clearly of IF we should respond and HOW. Are they telling others lies about you because they are having a moment of insecurity? Is their anger towards you because they are hurt by something you've said? Did you say something out of context? There are times I've said things or worded things that clearly could have been said differently and not have caused a situation to escalate and I had to apologize.

THE PRINCIPLES OF DEBBIE & GOLIATH

This is also a choice of picking your battles. Is it really an issue or is it an issue because you feel your way is better than theirs, when really it doesn't matter? There are a million scenarios that arise and we get to choose how to respond. We are created to FEEL and it is not a bad thing to have feelings but it is our responsibility to learn how we express them and when to share our feelings.

When I was a teenager, there was a lot of girls around my age in our neighborhood. I was quite the tom boy. I am the 8th of 9 kids and I have 6 older brothers. I was out there playing micro machines in the dirt, catching crawdads in the canal, and playing basketball until it was time to go in for the night. Naturally, having 6 brothers, I was mainly around boys!

Sadly, this made me a target for drama with the girls. One girl especially was so rude. She would come up to me at lunch, grab my drink and pour it all over my food. She lived particularly close to me on the same street. At first, I just shrugged it off and went on with life. I wasn't a very confrontational kid; I wasn't quiet but I wasn't confrontational. This girl was also about 2x my size in 6th grade. So... I just rolled my eyes and went on with life. Sadly, because she acted this way, she did not have many friends but oddly she was the one who always had a "boyfriend."

However, I want to focus on one aspect for now. This girl was rude, she was verbally abusive to others, and her actions weren't kind. You can only handle so much until you break. Well, that day I broke—I thought I was going to be grounded for the remaining time I lived at home. This certain day, she had been rude to a few of us at school already and then after school we had church activity for the girls where we met and had ladies there who would teach us certain things.

This day, the lady who taught us was late getting home from work so we were all just sitting on her porch waiting and here comes walking up to the steps our not so kind acquaintance. But she had an agenda! Immediately, she started going into it and talking about us all, saying things about our hair, our clothes and how I didn't wear make-up and so on....

HABITS OF SUCCESS

We had had enough at school and her coming to the activity just to keep it going wasn't cool. So, I mentioned I wasn't a confrontational kid but I also wasn't quiet. I stood up from the porch steps and blurted out something along the lines of, "At least we had friends who actually liked us and weren't desperate for affection that we'd kiss any boy!" I said it kind of fast... and... loud. I only had the courage to say it because there was the other 10+ girls sitting around me. This mean girl was stumped! She immediately went blank faced and then turned around and started crying. I felt bad, but I also knew I couldn't sit there and listen to her nonsense anymore. Well, one thing led to another, and we all stayed at the activity and went about our business. The mean girl was actually quiet for the most part!

So, the afternoon went on and dinner time comes. My back yard neighbor Sarah called my house. She was panicking. The mean girl and her mom showed up to her house to talk to her parents! Thankfully, they weren't home. They then went to another girl's house and her parents weren't home! Well, my parents weren't home either! All of our parents were actually at a church function together! Later on, somehow everyone ended up at my house! I'm pretty sure the other girls were pretty quick to let their parents know that I was the one who blurted out what I did.

So there we were in my living room. It ended up being 4 sets of parents, 4 girls, and The Mean Girl and her mom. It was awkward to say the least. As the mean girls mom starts off on how rude I was to her daughter and how could I say such things about her daughter and it hurt her feelings so much and she felt unwelcomed now.

My Dad, of all people, stood up and put his hand out and asked her to stop talking. He then turned to us girls and asked us to share our side. So, of course, the other girls were silent! I chimed in and started with how our day was at school. I explained how she poured my milk all over my food, made comments about all of our clothes, and so on. I even owned up to the fact that I called her desperate and how she always bragged about kissing boys.

After some back and forth, my Dad stood up again, looked at the mean girl's mom and said something along the lines of, "I think it's pretty clear here: our girls did not start this and while things could have been handled differently, words not have been said, your daughter's actions and words have put her in this situation to begin with. It would be wise to take a look at your parenting and home life." It was silent before but now it was dead silent. After those words seemed to register in the mother's brain, they quickly got up and left the house.

It was so bizarre and even thinking back on it now, my dad's words made such an impact on my life. We then were able to talk with our parents about possibly why this girl's behaviors were about. I learned by example that night not to react so quickly. It would have been so easy for me to get all defensive and upset because she was just flat out rude but having my Dad lead by example and seeing my Dad listen to both sides and not immediately get after ME for the things I said was lesson number one from that saga.

Seeing him then respond firmly, honest, and still in control of himself was number two. All of these 4 girls who sat in my living room learned valuable lessons that night. It didn't mean everything was perfect from then on, but I did learn to speak up. I didn't have to take it and I didn't have to be around it. She ultimately had a crush on one of my best friends who was a boy and she caused lots of drama by spreading rumors, but in the end, my character stood out and those who knew me, knew the truth.

I'm so thankful for my Dad and his example and trust in me. That night was the beginning of many talks and life lessons learned from my Dad in the short 18 years I had with him before he passed from cancer. I hold them close and cherish them. Emotional Intelligence will help you succeed in EVERY aspect of life. We have every right to FEEL all the emotions. We do not have every right to let those emotions guide our actions and impact others just because that's how we feel.

LAUREN COBB

About Lauren Cobb: Lauren Cobb is a wife to her amazing and supportive husband Tyler. A mother to 3 beautiful daughters who've taught her more in the last 12 years than she has learned in the first 23 years of her life.

At a young age Lauren knew she had a lot of ambition and drive. As she became an adult, she knew that entrepreneurship was her passion and thankfully married someone who supported that! Together with Ty they own a graphic and media design company that they've built from the ground up. Growing and seeing the successes from their own efforts has been one of the most rewarding experiences!

Self-development and leadership have been a big part of Lauren's life since she was 14. She traveled and taught leadership to youth across the country throughout her high school years. She knows first-hand how self-development is crucial to success in life. Knowing who you are and finding your purpose and passion is important.

As Lauren and her husband Ty are building their businesses and seeking a network and friends who are aligned with their values, they've found in Champion Circle and learned how to properly mastermind. Lauren is a member of the corporate executive team at Champion Circle Networking Association, founded and led by Jon Kovach Jr. Masterminds have changed her life and their business for the better.

Author's Website: *www.TyCobb.MyPortfolio.com*
Book Series Website: *www.ThePrinciplesOfDebbieAndGoliath.com*

LIZ SEARS
CREATE YOUR LIFE

If you want to change your world, change your mindset.

Mindset is one of those magical parts of life. Whether you're a young girl or an incredibly successful business owner running a billion-dollar company, your mindset creates your life experience. In 2021, I attended a conference with Tony Robbins called Business Mastery II. The ticket price for this event was $10,000 per ticket. One of the speakers at this event said his daily fee to consult a company was $70,000. Seventy-thousand dollars for one day of consulting them!

Then he said, "So, I was trying to think of what would be most beneficial to share with you today and decided that the most important topic I could discuss is mindset." Then he taught for the next hour about how your mindset determines everything:

- how you think,
- how you interact with others,
- how you plan,
- how you act,
- how you problem solve,
- how you experience life,
- the goals you set,
- the achievements you attain,
- everything.

Creating your life and your mindset go hand in hand. But before we go into that, let's start with a scenario and a bit of a trick question. Really take a moment to think about this question and come up with your answer before reading on:

> **Scenario:** A brother and sister are playing. Then the brother says something super mean to his sister, and she starts to cry. Their mom comes into the room and says to the brother, "You hurt your sister's feelings. Say you're sorry."
>
> **Question:** Who do you think is most hurt by what the mom just said, and why?

If you're like most people, you may answer that no one is hurt by what the mom said. She's just being a mom. You might answer that the brother is most hurt because he got caught or he realized that he hurt his sister's feelings or some other reason.

But, truly, it's the sister who is most hurt by what the mom said. And here's why: without meaning to, the mom just taught her daughter that someone else controls her feelings, not her. The mom has taught her daughter that she can't be happy unless her brother changes his behavior. If the little girl grows up believing that she can't be happy unless other people behave a certain way, then her happiness is always at risk and outside of her control. I don't know about you, but that's not the way I want to live. I prefer to be in charge of my happiness, and in here I'm going to share how you can be in charge of your happiness, too!

You may be wondering what the mom could have said instead. She could have just said, "That was a really mean thing to say. Say you're sorry." This way instead of saying that the brother controlled his sister's emotions, the mom is just pointing out what the brother did, and that he should apologize.

Whenever something happens, we have an emotional reaction. Sometimes our emotions tell us to feel happy or excited, and sometimes they can tell us to feel irritated, hurt, embarrassed, or angry. But just because our emotions tell us to feel a certain way doesn't mean we have to obey. Imagine if a stranger came up to you and said, "You have to feel really angry right now!" Your instant reaction would probably be more confused and wondering, "What's this guy talking about?" You'd definitely think he was really weird!

Our emotions are like that weird stranger who thinks he has the right to dictate how we're required to feel.

But the *most powerful moment of time* is in the space between our reaction and our response.

With the stranger, it's easy to not immediately feel "really angry." It's super easy to question what was just demanded of you. So, next time your emotions flare, try this. Instead of instantly and mindlessly obeying the command, *pause*. Don't act...yet—because this is where all of the power lies!

One of my most favorite quotes is by Viktor Frankl. He was a Jew during WWII and held as a prisoner in one of the most horrifying concentration camps. While he was in there, he was starved, humiliated, and tortured. As you can imagine, he had a LOT of emotional reactions. Most people would say he was absolutely justified in acting on those emotions. But during that time, Mr. Frankl realized the *most powerful moment of time*. He said,

> *"Between stimulus and response there is a space. In that space is our power to choose our response. In our response lies our growth and our freedom."*

He didn't view his emotional reaction as something that he *must* obey. Same for us! We don't have to view any of our emotional reactions as something we *must* obey.

There are two ways to live your life. You can live by reacting which is the same thing as obeying your emotions or you can live by creation.

The first step in creation is to decide what you want. Here are some things that I decided I want, and now I purposely frame my *responses* around these things:

HABITS OF SUCCESS

I want to be happy.

I want to be a good friend and have good friends.

I want to be my own best friend and talk to myself the way a best friend would.

I want to be the hero in my story. When things aren't going my way, I want to be like the hero in the movies who figures it out!

I want to be playful, confident, and kind.

I could keep going on, but you get the point.

So take a moment now, think about what you want, and make your own list. Imagine what your life would be like if you were able to *create* your own ideal life. I want you to dream with me for the next 21 days. I want you to pretend like you have the power to create a life you'll love and be SO excited to live! You are welcome to dream as big or small as you want for the next 21 days. Here's the **21-Day Dream Challenge**:

Step 1 - Setup
- Place a pen or pencil along with a pad of paper or a journal next to your bed.

Step 2 - Start
- When you wake up, do these things:
- Smile, think of how grateful you are to be alive, enjoy the feel of your blanket and pillow, and just feel gratitude while you smile. If you have hard things happening in your life, let this be your opportunity to pretend those things don't exist. Take a mental vacation from those problems and let this be a time just for you and your dreams.
- Then calm your mind, say a prayer if you pray, or just humbly expect your mind to be opened and to receive inspiration, and begin to think about what a perfect life would look like and feel like for you.

THE PRINCIPLES OF DEBBIE & GOLIATH

- Then, use what you placed next to your bed and begin writing a list of what you want in your life.
  - Don't look back and read what you wrote before. Always start a brand-new list each day. Some things will repeat, and some will be brand new.

Step 3 - Schedule
- After you've done this for 21 days, schedule a time to be alone to evaluate what you've written. You'll want to set aside about an hour where you can be uninterrupted and focused.

Step 4 - Evaluate
- Before you start to evaluate, first smile, feel gratitude, calm your mind, say a prayer if you pray, or just humbly expect your mind to be opened and receive inspiration.
  - The goal of evaluating your lists is to make a single list that makes you feel excited and connected to what you've written down.
- Now that you're ready, read through your lists.
- Take note if something you wrote down is similar to something else you wrote down. Group those answers together and then write a single phrase to represent each group.
- Take note if you wrote something that touches your heart or resonates with you. Draw a star or heart next to those.
- Decide if there's anything you wrote down that doesn't get you as excited. Then, feel comfortable drawing a line through those things because they don't make your final list...at this time. Maybe they'll make the list later, but for now, it's okay to leave those off.

Step 5 - Finalize
- Now that you have your single list, write it out and put it somewhere you'll see every day. You may even want to make

multiple copies of this and put them in different places so you can see it throughout the day.

This list is *your* Life Plan. Treat it like your guide. Use this list to help you make decisions including how to respond to each and every situation you find yourself in.

When my mom was a young girl, her life was pretty tough. Her mom was a school teacher who didn't get home from work until well after my mom and her brother got home from school. Her dad was an alcoholic who worked the night shift and would still be sleeping when they got home from school. She told me about how they had to go straight to their bedrooms when they got home from school and be perfectly quiet until he woke up. She would usually just do her homework at that time since there wasn't much else to do. This was back before cell phones, computers, or anything. I can't even imagine how bored she would be sometimes! Her dad was also pretty cruel and abusive to her brother and it broke her heart to witness that because there was so little that she could do to help.

My mom told me about her favorite TV show she used to watch called "Leave It To Beaver." She loved this show so much because she would dream of having a family who treated each other with love, kindness, and playfulness like that one day. My mom not only dreamed of having that one day, but she committed to making it happen. At a very young age, she decided that she was going to make that become her life no matter what her life was like to start with.

I remember how I felt each time my mom told me that story. I remember feeling that it doesn't matter what my circumstances might be, I'm not stuck. If there's something in my life I don't like, I can change it. I might have to work hard. I might have to wait until I'm older, but I can change and create anything I want with my life. And you can, too!

If you don't want to do the full 21-Day Dream Challenge, do a 14-Day or even a 1-Day Dream Challenge. Just start! Just dream! Knowing what you want is the foundation of creating your life. I'm excited to share with you the next steps in creating your life in the second book of this series. Until then, *dream* and begin creating *your* beautiful, ideal life!

LIZ SEARS

About Liz Sears: Liz Sears lives her life in every way to fulfill her life mission which is to "inspire the masses to live lives full of connection, contribution, adventure, and impact." As a speaker and writer, she focuses on the consistency of striving towards becoming the best version of ourselves and sharing how to be awake and engaged in life. She fully believes that life, with its extensive variety of obstacles and opportunities, can be an amazing adventure. It's all about how we play the hand we were dealt, and what we choose to create.

Liz has been married to her best friend since 1996 and together they have raised four wonderful sons. She is a proud alumna of Kent-Meridian High School and pursued Business Administration/Management at the University of Utah. Her roots trace back to Seattle Washington, but she and her family now call Layton, Utah home.

Beginning in the financial industry in 1995, Liz's career path has included roles such as Mortgage Loan officer, Property Manager, Real Estate Investor, and most recently as Broker/Owner of My Utah Agents. She has served many times in leadership roles in the Real Estate industry including on the Board of Directors for the Northern Wasatch Association of Realtors and as a Governing Board Member of the Women's Council of Realtors Utah.

Author's Website: *www.UtahsEliteRealtors.com*

Book Series Website: *www.ThePrinciplesOfDebbieAndGoliath.com*

HABITS OF SUCCESS

LORNA SHERLAND

SELF-ACTUALIZATION: THE LAYERS BUILT ON TRUTH

Life's adversities and challenges can be overwhelming, can't they? For many of us, particularly during our formative years, they're punctuated by feelings of inadequacy. For me, this ever-present sense of not being 'good enough' was both a constant companion and a shadow that followed me.

Taking a trip down memory lane to my high school days, this sentiment wasn't merely an occasional visitor; it took up residence within me. It's quite astonishing how moments from our teenage years can leave lasting imprints on our psyche. High school, often dubbed a microcosm of the larger world, taught me bitter lessons about exclusion. I felt as though an invisible barrier separated me from a particular group of girls. To them, academic prowess and socioeconomic privilege were more than mere markers—they were identities. Experiencing this exclusion only intensified my internal feelings of inadequacy, casting a long shadow on my self-esteem and influencing the trajectory of my relationships.

One of the major lessons from my self-introspective journey was the realization of the monumental impact of early-life perceptions on our self-worth and worldview. Today, as I advocate for personal growth and development, I firmly believe that young minds should be introduced to certain grounding concepts earlier in life. The idea of Chakras, for instance, which revolve around human energy and centers of balance, could be a guiding force for them. I often muse on moments of doubt I had, like the time I felt utterly out of place in my school uniform. It might sound trivial, but such seemingly minor events can have profound implications, shaping our self-perception and casting doubts on our self-identity.

One metaphor that has deeply resonated with me is that of "the layers we tell ourselves." Every person is a complex tapestry of experiences, beliefs, and emotions, and to truly evolve, one needs to peel back these layers of each category, one by one. One such peel back was a pivotal moment in my personal and professional journey was when I shifted the narrative of my business. I transitioned from advocating for concepts of freedom to championing empowerment. This wasn't just a business decision—it was a reflection of my own journey of introspection, understanding, and growth. I continued to peel!

Recently, I made a commitment that represents so much more than just a physical transformation—I pledged to lose 18 pounds by December 30th, as part of the challenging 75 hard program, a program of mental fortitude. While the objective is tangible, the implications run deep. It's about reaffirming my commitment to myself, understanding the layers of my resilience, and redefining my self-worth. Each time I face an obstacle, be it a moment of weakness or a break in the journey, I see it as an opportunity. An opportunity to reflect, recalibrate, and rise with even greater determination.

At the heart of my experiences and insights lies a powerful triad of perception, choice, and resilience. Through life's myriad challenges, I've come to view them not as insurmountable walls but as gauges of inner strength. I distinctly recall a speaking engagement centered around the power of choice. Even though I felt my delivery wasn't as poignant as I'd have liked it to be, that engagement remains a cornerstone in my journey toward self-awareness.

Confronting the ghosts of the past, navigating the murky waters of feelings of inadequacy, and harnessing the transformative power of choice and resilience have all been waypoints on my journey towards self-actualization. It's been a tumultuous yet enriching odyssey, and I am determined to continue pushing boundaries. My hope is that by sharing these deeply personal insights and experiences, I can light a beacon of hope, inspiration, and empowerment for others, encouraging them to embark on their personal journeys of self-discovery and growth.

LORNA SHERLAND

About Lorna Sherland: Lorna Sherland is a distinguished Mindset Leadership Transformation Coach at Freedom LifeStyle, where she specializes in helping driven female entrepreneurs overcome limiting beliefs to achieve six- and seven-figure milestones in their businesses to create time and money freedom. Lorna combines her extensive experience in real estate with her passion for empowering others, focusing on educating buyers and sellers to enhance their real estate experiences while empowering female entrepreneurs to go to the net level of growth and impact. As the founder of Success Power Brokers Real Estate and Consulting Services, with over 22 years of industry experience, Lorna has established herself as a Real Estate Mega Agent, successfully closing over 1,000 deals. Her philosophy is centered around the belief that a well-informed buyer or seller is the best consumer of her services. This dedication to client education has set a high standard in her field.

Lorna's journey in real estate began as a Broker in Newburgh, New York, where she committed to serving her clients far beyond their expectations, transferring her philosophy into practice. Additionally, she is a savvy Real Estate Investor, motivated by the goal of building wealth and creating a lasting legacy for her family, a principle she aligns with her biblical values. Her academic background includes a bachelor's degree in finance, which has been instrumental in her successful career. Since August 2018, Lorna has dedicated herself to mindset empowerment and transformation coaching.

Lorna's impact extends beyond her professional achievements. She is a thought leader in the industry, frequently speaking on topics such as buyer and seller dynamics, real estate trends, mindset resets, and homeownership. Her insights and guidance continue to inspire and transform the lives of many, particularly female entrepreneurs aspiring to reach new heights in their business endeavors.

Author's Website: *www.LornaSherland.com*

Book Series Website: *www.ThePrinciplesOfDebbieAndGoliath.com*

M. A. FULTS
GIANTS AMONG US

Encountering my first GIANT at the age of 12 was traumatic, painful, and left never-forgotten memories of the time and circumstances. Ultimately, however, it was a VICTORY. The year was 1970, and it began with joy, singing, peace, and new-found faith. First, my mother, Alice, then my brother, Steve, and then I encountered the Living God, Father, Jesus, and the Holy Spirit, all evidenced by an in-filling of the Spirit and speaking in tongues. Pretty heavy for a young 11-year-old. For Steve it was even more exciting, at the age of 16 he became "on fire for Jesus" never hesitating to tell of God's love for him and his love for God. Mom settled into a closer relationship than ever; with a God she had given her life to almost four decades earlier. And I was excited, filled with joy and a new-found wonder—I could have a personal relationship with God who previously had been distant, hanging on a cross, up on a wall. Now, with all I'd seen, felt and experienced in those early months of 1970, I knew I would have God with me always.

We were living in Tucson, AZ, where Mom's parents had moved to in 1956 to help with Grandpa's health and be near the University of AZ for his youngest son. Mom's sister and family had also moved to Tucson, so there was a great deal of support for Mom while Dad, a sergeant in the Army, did a tour in Vietnam. Dad had come home for Christmas in '69, with few changes in family dynamics from when he'd left 8 months before, meaning my brother and I were still fighting and Mom was struggling with being on her own, working and taking care of two constantly bickering, and growing, children. After extending his tour,

HABITS OF SUCCESS

Dad came home again in the summer of '70, foregoing Christmas leave that year in order to do so. In that summer of 1970, though, the family dynamics were significantly changed.

Mom had found a new confidence, independence, and authority. She also became more loving, more forgiving, and definitely less stressed. Steve and I no longer constantly fought but instead were more considerate of each other, finding a way to peace between us. Having attended multiple large group gatherings with other charismatics, along with weekly local small group meetings, we had all become more familiar with what it means to be Spirit-filled—with having a personal relationship with God, Father, Jesus, and the Holy Spirit, and we cared for, prayed for, and were there for each other. And Steve, well Steve had found a Father's (Father-God) love that had totally changed his paradigm of the world and his interaction with everyone he encountered.

At almost 17, Steve was 6'-5", well over 240 lbs. and still growing. He was also so gentle and loving of all those around him that everyone was drawn to him. He was a "gentle giant", in every good sense of the phrase. We all found in him a son, brother or friend who saw and accepted us just as we were. And maybe the biggest change in all of us was a free-flowing love, that "flowed from deep within." That is the dynamic of what Dad came home to, taking him by surprise, because he was now an outsider. He liked 'most' of the changes he saw in us, but was not able to accept "that charismatic thing", and therefore he never fit it. This caused tension in our home, such that when he left to return to Vietnam, we all breathed a sigh of relief.

Life that fall season was filled with school, work, meetings, and church. Mom, an extraordinary musician, wrote and directed a Christmas Cantata at Grandma's church, and continued to participate in two choirs. Steve was teaching himself how to play guitar, with an idea of joining the worship team in the near future, and playing Rugby at Sahuaro High School where he was a sophomore. Grandma invited me to attend Bible Study Fellowship with her, a distinct privilege as I'd spent nine of my 12 years out of the United States, so I was getting to know her for the first time. Time, those days were filled with so much, yet they went by so fast.

THE PRINCIPLES OF DEBBIE & GOLIATH

Christmas was wonderful, with so many new friends in the charismatic community, many, many Christmas preparations, and so much anticipation of the celebration—it was Christmas after all! In addition, Garrett and Freya Martin (not their real names), a couple my parents had met at Dad's previous duty station in Teheran, Iran, came to stay and visit with their five children. As the couple took my room, and the children spread out throughout the house, I slept with Mom on Dad's side of the bed. To say the house was filled would be an understatement. But in truth, it was filled with laughter and stories, games and remembrances, and lots and lots of love—just an ordinary Christmas, though without Dad.

Before and after Christmas there were many outings: Old Tucson Movie Studios, Arizona Sonora Desert Museum, and the Saguaro National Monument. On the 28th of December, Garrett, who was a bowler, invited us to go bowling with his family. I'd never been but was eager to go and so was Steve; both moms decided to stay home. Steve invited his 'like-a-brother' friend and new Christian, Dennis, to go as well. Dennis had been a drug addict who, although older by a few years, Steve had led to know the loving, forgiving Savior so prevalent in Steve's life. But recently Dennis had been drawn back into drugs and Steve saw the bowling as a time they would be able to talk. Since Dennis was old enough to be an adult driver for Steve's Learner's Permit, the three of us got into our family's large Chrysler sedan, Steve driving, Dennis in the front passenger seat and I behind Steve, while Garrett drove himself and his five children.

The bowling was loads of fun for all of us. I bowled two games and was willing to stay for a third with my brother and Dennis, but Garrett wanted to get back and thought I should go with him. Steve, wanting time to talk with Dennis alone, agreed and I headed out with the Martins. I stopped at the door to look back, saw Steve wave, and returned the wave. About an hour and a half later, while getting ready for bed, Mom commented that she had expected Steve home by now. She went into the bathroom and when the phone rang asked me to answer it. It was Dennis' mom, could she talk to my mom, please?

The call didn't take long, but I could see it upset my mom. She said Steve and Dennis had been in an accident—an ambulance ran a red light, without sirens, and hit the driver's side full on – and they had been taken to Tucson Medical Center (TMC), 15 minutes from our house. Dennis had called his mom, asking her to get in touch so Mom could get to TMC as soon as possible. Garrett took Mom to the hospital while Freya stayed with me and the rest of the children. As they left Mom asked me to pray. I prayed. Mom called about an hour later and said Steve was gone and with Jesus now. I prayed some more. This time for a miracle.

DEATH is a GIANT we all must face, some sooner than others. But FEAR of DEATH, that's an even bigger GIANT that can and will debilitate, prevent, and even destroy our ability to function, maybe even to live. Within our new-found faith, which Mom, Steve, and I had come to embrace, DEATH we knew, had been conquered 2,000 years ago. But with Steve's sudden death, I faced FEAR of DEATH. At the age of 12, I now knew DEATH could come at any time, to any one. If I had had to face that Fear alone, I probably could not have conquered it so quickly. Which is true of David with Goliath, is it not? No, David didn't face FEAR of DEATH when he faced Goliath, his relationship with a loving God had shown him he need not fear DEATH. However, the truth he knew with a certainty was that he was not alone when facing DEATH, or a giant named Goliath—God was with him.

And that December of 1970 God was with each one of us. From Mom to family to friends, we all gathered round each other, comforting, praying, laughing when remembering, crying when remembering, but all together. Having the certainty of knowing Steve was with the Jesus he loved so very much, knowing we would one day see Steve again, knowing Father-God, Jesus, and the Holy Spirit had not abandoned us, but were there with us as the Psalmist says in Psalm 91, with *"His massive arms wrapped around us"*.

While there are too many examples to provide here of how God was with us, before, during and after Steve's death, perhaps the best is Dennis, the young man in the car when Steve was killed. Dennis told us what he saw. Because the Chrysler was so big, and he was not a big man, he was able to see the ambulance coming and squeeze into the foot well. He then looked up in time to see Steve turn and look toward the oncoming vehicle, but then he saw Steve smile. Dennis firmly believes Steve saw only Jesus, not the ambulance. I believe that, too. More miraculous was that, after witnessing the death and how everyone came together to share the love, joy, and sorrow, Dennis turned his life completely over to Jesus. He was soon leading other addicts out of addiction and into freedom in Christ Jesus.

Having faced and conquered that FEAR of DEATH GIANT in 1970, my 2012 diagnosis of Stage 2 Breast Cancer held no fear for me. And any time a doubt would arise as I battled the cancer, I would remember, DEATH is not my GIANT to fight, and PERFECT LOVE casts out ALL FEAR.

M. A. FULTS

About M. A. (MaryAlice) Fults: Born into an Army family, followed by 39 years in and working for the US Navy, means Fults spent many years traveling and living in foreign countries including four years in Teheran, Iran. She has a BFA in Drama Production from the University of AZ and an MS in Management from Naval Postgraduate School in Monterey, CA. After retiring for the second time in 2022, Fults continued pursuing lifelong learning while embarking on a new career as a Kingdom Entrepreneur, Heart Healer, and Life Coach. She has been blessed with one son.

Book Series Website: *www.ThePrinciplesOfDebbieAndGoliath.com*

MARIS SEGAL
DEAR WOMEN OF THE WORLD

In the age-old biblical story of David and Goliath, David, a career shepherd, faces the giant Goliath and, against all odds, defeats him with a slingshot. Ladies, we are an incredibly special half of the human race. Let's explore this theme from a "Debbie & Goliath" perspective. We are life-giving and intuitively great connectors of humanity from heart to heart. And sometimes life gets messy, and we get to embrace those moments and rise.

I am humbly writing this letter to You, women of every age, everywhere, to share some wisdom and foundational tools that have guided my life through the many times I have faced Goliath. I invite you to read on with a curious student mind, and a lens into your own life and the women and girls who rise with you in every area of your life.

From our earliest days even in the womb until our final resting, "Goliath Moments" occur in many forms in our personal and professional lives, some human made, and some nature made and some even self-made. These moments do not discern age, gender, culture, or location. Why refer to these as "moments?" Because they pass with time! You may have heard the old saying, "This too shall pass." No matter how large or small the challenge, obstacle, trauma, and drama may be, at any age, while these moments make an impact, they do not define us—unless we let them! Each presents an opportunity to grow.

In a twenty-four-hour day, we are in relationship with someone or something from the time we wake up in the morning until we sleep.

HABITS OF SUCCESS

Relationships can't be avoided, and each begins with a connection. In my work with my husband as executive mindset and relational leadership coaches, trainers, and consultants, we call this relationship immersion, the RFactor. So, it stands to reason that there will be bumps along the way, moments during our day, week, month, year that may go awry with those connections. We call these bumps "Goliath Moments" and sometimes, we get in our own way with our doubts, and fears.

When we stand up as Debbie against Goliath, the "slingshot" referred to in this biblical story is a great metaphor for key "tools" we can use to be a victor in any Goliath Moment at any stage and age of our lives. *Mindset, Respect, Responsibility, Reframing and Resilience* are the cornerstones that when working in sync will build and maintain skills for a harmonious life that drive prosperous personal and professional relationships and support anything that may arise.

MINDSET

Our most important relationship connection begins with ourselves! We are the one relationship we can't leave home without! From our youngest years, the importance of a positive mindset and self-esteem are the lens that we see and lead our lives through minute by minute. We operate from the inside out. How we feel about ourselves and the messages we tell ourselves are how we show up in the world and how we treat others at work, school, and at home. It's important to feed positive messages into our brains on a regular basis. One way is by acknowledging and celebrating ourselves and our wins every day. This creates positive evidence and examples that feed our mind and influences our mindset and emotions.

I was a kid who never felt like I belonged. The youngest of ten cousins, even in my close Jewish family, I spent more time with the adults. I was small for my age and picked last for team activities. My two older sisters were national and international ranked water skiers and I feared I could never live up to them, so while my petite size helped me excel as a show skier with them, I chose not to compete—fear won.

Challenged by reading and numbers, I lived consumed by self-doubt, afraid to speak up and be wrong in class and group settings. I never raised my hand first! I remember the panic that used to set in as a question came from the teacher in front of the class. Teachers regularly told my parents that, while I was not a great student, I worked well with others, was inquisitive, intuitive, and great at making everyone feel heard and included. This is where I found my voice and purpose of supporting and empowering others which has become my life's work. My lack of self-confidence inside kept me small and feeling distant outside and that's how I was treated. Remember, if you are out of sorts and feeling negative, it's likely that those around you may think you're in a "mood" and will treat you that way.

CHOICE MINDSET

How we approach the Goliath Moments in our lives is always our choice. The "choice mindset" to F.A.C.E. (Freely Acknowledge Current Emotion) describes the challenge and how we view the situation, which can be the difference between thriving or just barely surviving. When we recognize and F.A.C.E. Goliath head on, from a grounded belief, a knowing with faith that solutions exist, we can choose to "respond versus react." To respond, we take a breath and pause from a thoughtful place before jumping in to react emotionally.

A positive mindset prepares us deep Inside from a place of believing that "I can handle this." Conversely, we can also choose overwhelm, fear, and avoidance, which is guaranteed to lead to defeat. "Choice is the bridge between imprisoning or freeing ourselves from the challenging moment." Science has proven that our brains can only process one thought, one choice, at a time.

So, why not make it positive! We were put on this planet with purpose and it's crucial to recognize your worth and value as an individual. Surround yourself with loving and trusted support. Know that you are worthy and have the power within to embrace your unique qualities, talents, and strengths. Sometimes easier said than done. "The choices we make all day, determine our future!"

HABITS OF SUCCESS

RESPECT is a fundamental birthright and life skill that will shape your relationships and interactions with others. First begin with respecting yourself! "Treat yourself the way you want others to treat you." Respect offers a grounding for facing anything that comes your way.

RESPONSIBILITY will empower you to take charge of your life by embracing opportunities to make wise choices and stand accountable for your actions. One way to avoid potential "Goliath Moments" at work or home is to be clear in your communication with others so that expectations are in agreement.

REFRAMING can help you embrace the power of perspective from a place of gratitude, not judgement. Be present to others' perspectives, listen, and meet them where they are. With a curious mind, ask yourself, "what can I gain/learn from this moment/this person," or "this could have been worse." When we reframe, shifts happen.

RESILIENCE is the ability to accept and bounce back from setbacks, and failures. After all, life is full of ups and downs, and inevitable change. Understand that setbacks are not permanent and remember, "this too shall pass." Resilience occurs when we seek and accept support from others. It's not about avoiding difficulties but rather about F.A.C.E.-ing them head-on with determination and perseverance.

Years ago, I was in Afghanistan as a strategic advisor working with an NGO (Non-Governmental Organization). I felt a profound sense of responsibility to show up for them and be in service. The children living at the center, school age boys and girls, were there because their mothers were in prison, mostly for committing crimes to protect themselves and their children against their violent husbands and families. Their children, and in particular daughters, had been subjected to horrific physical acts, sold into marriages at very young ages, rape, and mutilation and acid attacks leaving them not only marred physically but also emotionally distrusting, sad, angry, heart-broken, and lonely.

This center, hidden deep in the community away from the sites of the Taliban provided safety, education, and a sense of belonging for the youth. Having spent years working with underserved and marginalized children across the U.S. and the globe, I was struck by the universal sound of laughter in the yard where they played. We paired up the students and each were given a camera. We guided them to photograph each other sharing themes and emotions: play, jump, sit, happy, sad, joyful.

One young girl, whose face and arms were acid burned sat on a swing alone with the camera in her hand. Her brownish-green eyes were hauntingly beautiful and deeply sad. I joined her on the swing and two other children came over. We each shared what we liked about ourselves to help encourage her and we photographed each other. She faced down staring at the ground and cried. I heard the translator's words and they cut through me like a knife. The young student replied, "I am broken, there is nothing to like about me."

By the end of the next day, she was connecting more one on one and when asked the same question, she faced me and said, "I like my eyes because they are beautiful and will always show me the way." From a place of fear and distrust, she shifted as we navigated with respect. She able to reframe and from this place she could grow stronger and resilient.

I have experienced and supported friends, family, colleagues, and clients facing their Goliath Moments from death and destruction to financial ruin, broken promises, earthquakes, and hurricanes. The likelihood is extremely low that there is anyone on the planet who has not faced Goliath Moments at least once in their life.

If I knew in my youth what I know now as an adult, my life may have been less fearful, less stressful, and I would have trusted myself more at a much earlier age. That said, I have no regrets and would not change a thing. Every joyful accomplishment and challenging moment has been meant for me as a gift to grow that I continue to unwrap with every new experience.

From a place of a positive Mindset, when we choose to show up with Respect, stand up and be Responsible, Reframe limiting beliefs and step forward with Resilience, we can F.A.C.E. Goliath Moments and navigate them with consistent action to be victorious. Imagine if every person on the planet took this approach in their personal and professional lives even for one week.

Each of us is a single star of brilliant light. We are all connected as humanity first and that's there the bottom line begins. May this letter inspire and empower you to be who you are authentically and confidently as you prosper and thrive at home, work, and in your community.

MARIS SEGAL

About Maris Segal: Maris Segal coaches, consults, and collaborates with executives, entrepreneurs, celebrities, and rising leaders to identify and bring their professional, personal, and philanthropic vision to life. Maris' focus on evolving human relation skills leverages her relationship marketing and mindset expertise with the power of "head and heart leadership" to build a peak performing culture of connected, confident individuals and teams for maximum impact. Often referred to as "America's Master Connectors," working alongside her husband Maris and Ken live by the philosophy that "We are all connected as human's first and that's where the bottom line begins." As authors, their book, The RFactor, a story of evolving relationships sits at the core of their work. In addition, Ken and Maris are sought-after speakers on stages, live events, and podcasts. They have been TEDx speakers and featured authors in 15 business and leadership-centered books.

Over four decades across thirty countries, she has served a wide spectrum of local and global leaders, brands, and policy makers. From board rooms and classrooms to Harvard, Super Bowl Halftimes and Papal events, Ken and Maris are also award-winning event producers known for uniting diverse populations with innovative cross-cultural marketing and personal development programs that bring a creative voice to issues, causes and brands. As certified Executive and Relationship coaches, they set a path for every client to build high performing businesses and elevate personal and professional leadership for maximum impact and a 360-degree thriving life! For a free RFactor Gratitude Practice Guide visit *www.SegalLeadershipGlobal.com*. Connect with Maris - Info@SegalLeadershipGlobal.com

Author's Website: *www.SegalLeadershipGlobal.com*

Book Series Website: *www.ThePrinciplesOfDebbieAndGoliath.com*

HABITS OF SUCCESS

> I raise up my voice—not so that I can shout, but so that those without a voice can be heard. ... We cannot all succeed when half of us are held back.
>
> ~ Malala Yousafzai

HABITS OF SUCCESS

MEL MASON
CHAOS BEFORE THE CALM

"Enter at your own risk" is the sign that should have hung on the bedroom door of my thirteen-year-old self, warning you about what was to come. If you didn't know any better, you would've thought a bomb went off when you walked in. My entire floor was covered. Not only was the floor completely hidden with my stuff, but I also had trash strewn all over the place. Most people have paths to get from one area to another. In my room, there were no paths. There was just clutter everywhere!

The only time my room ever got cleaned was when my mom would get frustrated enough to do something about it. And she would do a really good job getting it organized. Everything would have a place and be in its place. All the surfaces would be clean and dusted. The floor was vacuumed. But here's the thing. Anytime she would clean it, in no time at all my room would go right back to the way it was before she put all that hard work in. What I didn't realize at the time was my external environment was a mirror reflection of what was happening on the inside of me. Because on the inside, I was littered with clutter too! I was carrying around lots of stuck emotions that I didn't know what to do with and operating from the limiting stories I made up about myself as a result of all of my life experiences.

At this point in my life, I couldn't have cared any less about what my room looked like, because I didn't even care whether I lived or died. Quite frankly, I was trying to get out of this human suit and off the planet. I was reckless. I put anything I could get my hands on, that would change the way I thought and felt, into my body to numb out and disconnect. And I often found myself praying that whatever combination I was ingesting would just kill me and put me out of my misery.

HABITS OF SUCCESS

My early years were extremely dark and traumatic. I came into the world thinking I was an accident. My parents used protection, but it didn't work, so growing up I was told that I was a hole in the condom. Because of that, I always felt like I was a burden and to blame for anything that didn't go right. Especially my parent's divorce. I believed that if I wasn't born, maybe they would still be together. I also came into the world thinking I was a thief and a horrible person because my mom lost her teeth when she was pregnant with me and told me that it was my fault, because I stole her calcium.

As the years went on, my life experience didn't get any lighter or easier. By the age of eight years old, I was sexually abused multiple times by two different people in my life. One of them was a neighbor and the other person was my older brother. I learned that my body was not my own. That it was for the pleasure of others. I also learned not to trust the people closest to me. I felt like I didn't matter. I felt like an object. I hated being in my skin and I hated being alive.

Then one day my mom's high school friend started taking me to Pioneer Club at the local Baptist Church. I was a sponge. I was looking for answers. I was looking for meaning in my life. As soon as I understood what it meant, I accepted Jesus Christ as my Lord and Savior, got baptized and began the long process of healing all the pain I carried within, the inner clutter. I became a beacon of light in the church, ministering to others and supporting them in their journey to accept Jesus into their hearts.

The greatest gift I received from that part of my journey was knowing that every painful experience I went through wasn't for nothing. It wasn't just for me to suffer and live a miserable life. I learned that God had a plan for my life. He had a plan to use it for good and that all my pain would someday be a benefit to others. I just had no idea what that would look like. Knowing that my experience would someday benefit others was often the only thing that kept me alive. It was the only thing that kept me going and willing to walk through the hurt and suffering to eventually heal, so that I could share my story with others.

So, what I want to you leave you with today is this. I want you to know that you matter. I want you to know that God has a plan for your life. It's not your job to know what it is. It's your job to trust that He's got you. He has the 30,000-ft perspective. You only have the sea level view. No matter what you are going through in life, God has a plan. God has your back. Everything is for your growth and for your highest good, no matter how painful it is. No matter how dark it may seem right now.

Think of a seed that gets planted in the earth. It's dark. There is no light. And the only way for it to grow is for it to crack through its shell and shoot up through the darkness, not knowing if it is ever going to reach the light. Then one day it finally breaks through and blooms for all of us to see and appreciate. But without the darkness, there would have been no beauty.

I would have never imagined that God would use my experience to support people in clearing the clutter in their lives, but He did. I have been blessed to work with hundreds of clients that struggled with clutter like I did. All because I was willing to do the work and heal. My willingness to get to the root of my own clutter has made it possible for me to support others in doing the same. I'm able to make a difference for people because I've been there. I understand what it's like to want to stay hidden behind the walls of stuff. I understand what it feels like to not feel safe with members of your family that you are supposed to be able to trust.

My journey of healing has led me to become The Clutter Expert. I now support people in getting to the root of why and how the clutter accumulates, so that it doesn't keep coming back. And the best part about what I do is that when you clear the clutter at the core, when you get to the cause, not only do you create order in your life effortlessly and spontaneously, but every other area of your life gets better too. Your relationships get stronger, you get healthier, you experience increased abundance financially, you have more energy than you know what to do with, and so much more!

Want to find out exactly how every area of your life gets better? Then be sure to grab volume two of this series when it comes out!

Dedication: To my niece Makayla Rose Deshais. You are my heart and my joy. I'm so proud of you! Stay loving and gentle. Love, Auntie Mel

MEL MASON

About Mel Mason: International, Best-Selling Author, Mel Mason is The Clutter Expert, and as a sexual abuse survivor, she grew up depressed, suicidal, and surrounded by clutter. What she realized after coming back from the brink of despair and getting through her own chaos was that the outside is just a mirror of the inside. And if you only address the outside, the clutter keeps coming back. That set her on a mission to empower people around the world to get free from clutter inside & out, so they can experience happiness and abundance in every area of their lives.

Author's Website: www.DeclutteringSpaces.com

Book Series Website: *www.ThePrinciplesofDebbieAndGoliath.com*

DR. ONIKA SHIRLEY
NOT QUALIFIED

"Don't allow critiques from unqualified people to stop you from living the life of your dreams."
~ **Dr. Onika Shirley**

In life, people will try to critique you when they are not qualified, but it's important that we know who we are and what we're capable of bringing to the table. I learned that feeling confident in myself might depend on the situation, but it was yet in my control. For instance, we can feel very confident in some areas of our lives, such as our careers, but lack confidence in other areas, like relationships. Our confidence levels rarely have anything to do with our actual abilities but based on our personal perceptions. Our perception has to do with how we think about ourselves and what we think others are thinking about us; however, these thoughts can be flawed. As I worked on my self-confidence. I had to believe in my abilities, I had to believe that there's a higher power that resides within me. I was willing to move on to what was positive and look at what was negative, and then work on what needs to be worked on and overlook what's said and done to be hurtful versus helpful.

As a woman, I feel we as women deserve to win in every area of our lives and it's time that we conquer the giants of spiritual health, physical flaws, financial wealth, and emotional deficiencies. It could be very hard for a woman to slay her giants in a man's world, but it's not impossible. We can do it. When we as women actively and consistently support one another, it can be done. Now I love how the world defines women's empowerment and how it can be developed. In the secular world, a woman can be empowered by equipping her with knowledge, providing her with useful resources, and by giving her worldly opportunities to understand her self-worth. While the world's view certainly resonates, I think it's vital that we encourage ourselves and other women of faith to also seek empowerment in Christ.

In the word of God, it tells me that empowerment comes from Him. The word of God also helps me to realize that power, identity, and strength come from Him and Him alone. My power, my identity, and my strength don't come from the one that gives worldly promotions and positions. In 2 Corinthians 12:9 it reads, "But he said to me, 'My grace is sufficient for you, for my power is made perfect weakness.' Therefore, I will boast more gladly of my weaknesses, so that the power of Christ may rest upon me," and Isaiah 40:31 reads, "But those who trust in the Lord will find new strength. They will soar high on wings like eagles. They will run and not grow weary. They will walk and not faint." Once I understood where my empowerment came from, I can now lead other women to a well of power, love, and soundness that never runs dry.

Me Foundation

After having two car accidents at the age of nineteen, I had to accept and trust myself while seeking to have a sense of control in my life at a time that seemed to be out of control. I had to have a positive view of myself in this negative situation. I didn't just have two car accidents where I could say I walked away unharmed or with a few scratches, but the reality is I couldn't. The results of those car wrecks of November 1995 and March 22, 1996, were almost two months in the hospital, a broken jaw, the loss of my two front teeth, a lost left femur, a crushed knee, broken toes twice, crutches for a year, a limp, and scars for a lifetime. I had a long road to recovery physically and mentally. I had to believe in myself, and I couldn't allow the physical scars to determine my ability to face the giants of this world. Building strong confidence muscles is something that we can all achieve with enough time, focus, and practice. Trauma could cause one to question their ability to function in the world; however, it was important for me to know that I was not alone and that I had a family that supported me. I couldn't allow the opinion of others to determine my ability to do or not to do. I think it was important for me to mention the two car accidents because as I entered a career, in manufacturing the impact of those car accident could've questioned my ability to perform. I had a boss that told me I couldn't do a certain job because of my leg and my response to him was please don't place a limit on me. If I can't do it, I will tell you, but I wasn't going to allow his opinion to stop me from doing what I knew I was willing to work on. That giant was brought down. I know he didn't mean any harm because he was a great help to me along the way to obtain the position I desired, but if I had allowed what he said to stop me I wouldn't have started the career of my thoughts. As time passed, I was not small and insignificant but at one point ran everything except maintenance. I did some brave, skillful, and important stuff that made a difference in my life and the lives of others.

As a woman thinks, so is she... I had thoughts of success long before I started to work for my unnamed company—I started with the company in 2007, eleven years after those life-changing car accidents. My thoughts, words, and actions made all the difference in the world. It took me empowering myself to push through some of the most painful days of my life. I knew my strengths and I didn't deny my weaknesses and I had a positive view of myself in this negative situation. I couldn't afford to be doubtful, passive, and submissive to my circumstances. I set realistic and achievable goals in incremental stages for where I was at the time. Sometimes we must slow down and think logically about a situation.

I want to share six practical ways to empower yourself. I have used these for years and honestly, these six things have empowered me to be the woman I am today. I am one that slays giants, and I am proud about elevating other women to do the same. Are you ready to be empowered?

6 Practical Ways To Be Empowered

1. I prayed. Prayer is practical. I took my concerns to the Lord in prayer. I asked for guidance, strength, and my breakthrough.
2. I used words of affirmation. I reminded myself daily that I was beautiful and wonderful made and that "pleasant words are a honeycomb and sweet the soul and healing to the bones" Proverbs 16:24

HABITS OF SUCCESS

3. I committed time to read the word of God to renew my strength. I discovered for myself that as I was fighting for a life I had an all-powerful God fighting on my behalf.
4. I held myself accountable. I had to be responsible for my actions and inactions. I had to hold myself to a higher standard than my condition as well as the expectations of others. Sometimes people can hinder your life's progress by giving you a pass where you need to be active.
5. I had to be vulnerable. People need to know that you're an overcomer of something and the joy and peace you now have were once feelings of overwhelm and uncertainty.
6. I supported others while I healed. The quickest way to overcome a personal situation is to help others overcome theirs. I was committed to helping others while I healed myself.

We sometimes tend to confuse inexperience with unqualified. You can learn anything. I had learned a lot, so I immersed myself in a company and its products, and my career took off. The bottom line to slay your giants you must work on you. When you work on you can work on anything.

> *"God has appointed the giants of your life with the intention of overcoming them for you and teaching you to rely on Him through them."*
> ~ Adam Houge

As you go through life, remember you were created with and for a purpose. The small can defeat the large. Everything you're becoming was seen in childhood. You have always been brave, resourceful, and resilient. People around will give you a chance to take on a task that seems to be too big for you, yet you will succeed, and your bravery will come from your confidence that you're fighting for God's honor and that God is on your side. For me, I always look at what I do through the lens of it's for the people's good but for God's glory. Don't allow the opinions

THE PRINCIPLES OF DEBBIE & GOLIATH

of others to make you feel small and insignificant and don't be paralyzed by the fear of having to face a giant.

I am dedicating this chapter to my niece, Shanell Thomas.

DR. ONIKA SHIRLEY

About Dr. Onika L. Shirley: Dr. Onika L. Shirley is from Helena- West Helena, Arkansas. She is the Founder and CEO of Action Speaks Volume, Inc. She is a Procrastination Strategist and Behavior Change Expert and is known for building unshakable confidence, stopping procrastination, and getting your dreams out of your head into your life. She is a Master Storyteller, International Speaker, Serves in Global Ministry. Dr. Onika has worked in manufacturing for the last sixteen and half year where she has held several leadership positions including production operations manager. During her time as production operations manager, she actively worked on creating an environment of unity and a place to work on one accord working towards the same mission and vision. She worked to be more productive while having key members hold themselves accountable for their areas of responsibility. Dr. Onika was an advocate for professional development and ensured her team as well as herself conducted weekly and monthly trainings. Dr. Onika is an International Best-Selling Author, International Award Recipient, Serial Entrepreneur, and Global Philanthropist who is impacting lives in the USA, Africa, India, and Pakistan. She is a Motivational Speaker and Christian Counselor. Dr. Onika is the Founder and Director of Action Speaks Volume Orphanage Home and Sewing School in Telangana State, India, Founder and Director of Action Speaks Volume Sewing School in Khanewal and Shankot, Pakistan. She founded, operated, and visited an Orphanage home in Tuni, India for four years and she supported widows in Tuni, India. She is the founder of Empowering Eight Inner Circle, ASV C.A.R.E.S, ASV Next Level Living Program, and P6 Solutions and Consulting. She has served for 13 years as a therapeutic foster parent for the State of Arkansas.

Author's Website: *www.ActionSpeaksVolumes.com*

Book Series Website: *www.ThePrinciplesOfDebbieAndGoliath.com*

RACHEL CORPUS
EXTEND LOVE

The night before 5th grade started, I remember meeting the entity in my closet. He had yellow eyes and he smelled like eggs. My dog, Barney, would not come into the room. He would stand at my bedroom door and growl. I shut the door to my closet and hung my rosary on the doorknob. I heard one of my Angels say, "Remember what this felt like. You will feel this again tomorrow."

Well, super. Needless to say, I slept in the family room that night.

I was full of first-day butterflies the next morning! I found my locker and began to unwrap the magnetic mirror I talked my mom into buying. And then I felt the feeling from last night creep back in. It crept into my spine and belly like I had eaten something bad. I was about to be sick. Suddenly someone slammed my locker door on my hand. It was Calvin, the class bully. You could smell him before you heard him, and he was known for his appetite for meanness. The encounter shook me. And the smell reminded me of the night before-like rotten eggs.

That evening, when the sun when down, I heard more scratching in my closet. Again, my dog would not come into my bedroom. I ran over and shut the door. I hung the rosary. And this time I moved my heavy dresser in front of it. One more night in the family room.

The next day, the word RAT was written in black marker on all my new notebooks and folders. I could still smell the ink from the marker. In math class, I noticed that Calvin had black marker all over his hands. He turned right around and mouthed to me, I WILL KILL YOU.

It was ballet night, so I got home late. My room was already dark. I had to go into my closet. I opened the door, and everything seemed fine. I pulled the light on and hurried to pick out my clothes for the next day. Calvin's face showed up in my mind, mouthing I WILL KILL YOU with that smug grin. I was ashamed of myself. I just sat there and took it. I felt so weak and powerless. I felt so alone. As the anger bubbled up in me, the closet began to smell again, and the lights flickered. For a brief second, the lights went out, totally, and I saw two yellow eyes looking at me. I grabbed my clothes and ran out. Couch bed, once again, in the family room.

The next day I arrived at school to find a bag of dog poop in my locker. I took it to my teacher and told her the whole story. She listened and advised that I do my best to ignore him. This sent anger raging through my body. Later, Calvin found me on the way home and beat me up for telling on him. I knew I had to handle this on my own. But I am not a fighter, more violence didn't feel right. But honestly, I had no idea what to do.

When I got home that late afternoon, my closet door was open, and everything inside had been pulled out and thrown all over the room. My radio was on at full volume, playing only static. I had a small black and white TV at that time, and it, too, was on at full blast, just static. My closet was completely dark… too dark, I thought. No one else was home. I was alone, and there was no one to help me. My dog was nowhere to be found. I was going to handle this on my own.

I tried to turn off the radio and TV first, but they just kept turning back on. I pulled the chain in the closet, but the light would only flicker for a moment and go back to darkness. So, I stood in my room and yelled, "COME OUT. I'M HERE." Nothing. Nothing happened. I kicked the door to my bedroom. "WHAT'S WRONG? ARE YOU SCARED OF ME?" Still, nothing. My parents would be home soon.

THE PRINCIPLES OF DEBBIE & GOLIATH

I felt myself take a big breath, and my shoulders went back like I was filling the room. I knew what had to be done. I walked right into the closet and shut the door. It was black as night.

Standing in the darkness, I spoke softly. I didn't yell. I hated being yelled at. I felt myself sit down gently. I didn't like to be handled roughly. I could still hear the radio and TV on at full volume. I kept myself calm by tracing the seams of my jeans with my fingertips and counting to 100 over and over. And then, suddenly, silence. The radio and TV turned off at the same time. It's like there was an absence of sound. My ears began to ring. And my closet began to fill with the scent of beautiful, fresh roses. And then the yellow eyes appeared again in front of me. The entity spoke in a throaty, low, voice, "I need rest."

"I don't understand," I managed to say back.

It repeated, "I need rest."

I wasn't sure what to do. In my head, another voice spoke. I knew this voice well. It was one of my Guardian Angels. She said, "You know this feeling. This entity seeks kindness. That is all."

The yellow eyes were still looking at me, waiting for a response. I so desperately wanted to stand up and turn the lights on! I was a child, after all! But I pulled bravery into my heart and thought about what this might mean.

I asked, "Do you mean you're tired?"

"Yes."

"Do you want to sleep in my bed?"

"No, I want to sleep here. Can I?"

"You mean here, in my closet? On my clothes?"

"If I can, yes. I am alone."

HABITS OF SUCCESS

It's weird to say this, but I feel like it wasn't totally me answering. I feel like it was my Angels or God talking through me. Because I stopped being scared. All I felt was love. I heard myself say, "I am alone, too. You can stay here as long as you want. And then my Angels will show you the way home."

The closet became kind of iridescent at that moment, and I could see what he looked like. I was expecting to see a gnarly demon or beast. When In fact, this was a little boy wearing old-fashioned clothing: grey wool knickers, a cream-colored shirt with buttons and suspenders. He wasn't more than 8 years old. And then he said to me, "Your friend at school, the boy who hurts you so much…his father is mean to him. He scolds him and beats him with a board. He is alone like us."

And then the closet went peacefully dark. I slept in my own room that night. And I knew what I was going to do the next morning. If Calvin came after me, I was going to get him first. Beat him at his own game. If he can be mean, I can be meaner. If he can be scary, I can be scarier. I slept soundly.

The next morning before school, sure enough, Calvin came up to me, holding a big rock in his hand. He was telling me that he picked out this rock specially for me. He was going to use it to beat my head in after school. He was so close to me that his spit was hitting my lips. I felt my adrenaline pumping. I had prepared for this all night, and I knew it was either going to work or make things much worse. I backed up about five feet, took a big breath, charged as fast as I could toward him. He looked amused. Everyone else near the jungle gym stopped what they were doing and watched. It was go time.

My feet were flying and my heart was beating out of my chest. His ugly mug got more shocked as I got closer, and, right as I was about to tackle him right in his midsection, I felt my arms do something I did not want them to do. I HUGGED him. What the heck? And then I did it again! I wrapped my arms as tightly as I could around his stinky body and I hugged him as hard as I could! And he started laughing! The kids around us started to chant, Calvin and Rachel, sitting in a tree, K-I-S-S-I-N-G! Well, that snapped us right out of whatever it was! He pretty much left me alone after that. From that point forward I knew that if I could send a demon boy home, I could *certainly* handle a bully! And I didn't have to handle it with more violence.

Where there is anger, there is fear. When someone is hurting you, that person has been hurt. It doesn't excuse their behavior, but it may help you understand them. Feel your feelings. Don't push them down—even if they are so strong, they turn on all the electricity around you. When you reach out for help, people might not know how to help you. That's ok. Beloved, keep asking. And know that you have come to this earth fully equipped with everything you need (and more) to live a beautiful and successful life. Love yourself, sit with your beasts, and extend love to your enemies. And those abilities you have will wake up within you, little by little.

You are loved.

This piece is dedicated to Raya, Isabelle and Addy, and all the young women who battle beasts that try to make them small. You are here to change the world and I am grateful for you. Fill the Universe with your Light, just by being you.

~ Rachel

RACHEL CORPUS

About Rachel Corpus: Rachel Corpus is a psychic medium and Angel communicator who specializes in helping people connect with their highest purpose and connect to the Source of God Energy. Rachel connects with people on the other side, Angels, animals, Light beings, Starseeds, and a very special collective of extraterrestrials who call themselves SARAI. Rachel specializes in connecting through the quantum realm, the multiverse, parallel dimensions, and past/other lifetimes. You may find Rachel working with people on television, radio, large audiences, on her podcast, or working one-on-one with clients. Learn more by visiting Rachelcorpus.com.

Author's Website: *www.RachelCorpus.com*

Book Series Website: *www.ThePrinciplesOfDebbieAndGoliath.com*

RUTHE HAGE

EMBRACING LIGHT ON THE MENTORSHIP JOURNEY

"We need to reshape our own perception of how we view ourselves. We have to step up as women and take the lead."

~ Beyoncé

RUTHE HAGE

About Ruthe Hage: Ruthe Hage is a distinguished Mindset and Personal Development Coach, renowned for her ability to inspire and guide individuals toward unlocking their full potential and embracing their divine purpose. Based in Spring Creek, Nevada, Ruthe has dedicated her life to helping others illuminate their paths, drawing from her extensive experience and personal journey of transformation. Ruthe pursued a Bachelor of Education at the University of Nevada, Reno. Ruthe later transitioned into the financial world, where she worked closely with clients, helping them navigate their financial landscapes. Ruthe sought mentorship and guidance, finding it in the teachings of Brendon Burchard, Bob Proctor, and Sandy Gallagher.

Her experience being mentored by these influential figures was transformative, leading to profound shifts in all areas of her life. She has since become a Certified High-Performance Coach and Proctor Gallagher Consultant, dedicating her life to supporting others in their journeys towards personal and professional fulfillment.

Ruthe is the proud mother of three beautiful souls, a doting Nanna to two grandchildren, and blessed with two daughters-in-law. She is the founder of LUX Life Coaching, a platform through which she offers resources, support, and guidance to those seeking to brighten their lives and reach their fullest potential.

Author's Website: *www.msha.ke/RutheHage*

Book Series Website: *www.ThePrinciplesOfDebbieAndGoliath.com*

SALLY WURR
DO YOU KNOW WHERE YOU ARE GOING TO?

This is a question I have asked myself in some form since about the age of 5 years old. Now I am asking you. You chose to read this book either by happenstance or it was recommended to be a great resource. As you move through these critical stages of your life, I want you to remind yourself to question why you are doing or saying something. And is it in your current and future best interest? In other words, does it take you to where you want to go or where someone else wants you to go?

You can never have enough resources to help you make decisions. It is never just one idea; we build our inner selves and opinions based on the things we are exposed to. Be open to hearing many sides to a story or journey.

If someone you like and respect shares their thoughts with you, you will most likely listen more closely than if it is someone you do not like or trust.

When I think back to when I was 13 years old, I had already formed opinions on many things. I was in the sixth grade and was one of the oldest students in the class. My skill sets were better developed than most of the other students. I believe this is one of the reasons the teachers always saw me as a leader.

HABITS OF SUCCESS

I was a quiet student and did not really interact unless I had something to say. I kept to myself and did what was right for me, not what everyone else was doing. Which made me look different than those who were trying to grab the limelight. They wanted the limelight, but I did not. I was always happy to be going down my own trail. Do not be afraid to do this yourself, if it fits your personality.

I have found that it does not matter what age you are, there will always be someone to criticize something. Ignore them the best you can, unless you value their interpretation of your life.

Your early teenage years are at the cusp of your adolescence, a crucial phase of personal development. It's the perfect time for you to be introduced to the concept of setting life goals, helping you to envision your future, and providing you with tools to make informed decisions. I'd like to explore and explain some strategies that can help guide you on this path. I say this with utmost authority as I was a young lady once.

The best place to begin is by reflecting on what you've already done and the things that interest you.

- Explore your interests.
- Figure out what gives you joy.
- Determine your personal values.
- What makes you happy?
- What are you good at?
- What are you not so good at?
- What do you find to be meaningful in your life?

These are the foundations for setting goals that align with your authentic self.

One of the most important items is to set specific goals for yourself. Goals that you can measure and see where you are at in the progress.

THE PRINCIPLES OF DEBBIE & GOLIATH

Define what success means to you. For example, you might want to become a pediatrician or a published author. Both life paths require skills that you may or may not have. Help yourself be successful in your endeavors by knowing what you are best suited for.

I think it's better to set short- and long-term goals in life. The earlier you learn how to set goals the much easier it is as an adult. By setting short-term goals for yourself for the near future it helps you breakdown the things that you want to do in short steps. It also teaches you how to prioritize and keep focused on those goals. For example, if it's important for you to get good grades then my guess is you focus and you put steps in place for you to achieve those good grades. If you know next year you want to try out for the cheerleading squad or the debate team, there are steps involved to prepare you to take on those goals.

A process that I was taught as an adult and wished I had learned it as a younger me is called S.M.A.R.T. Goals. S.M.A.R.T. Goals are an acronym that means goals that are Specific, Measurable, Achievable, Relevant, and Time-bound. When you're setting goals, these are some of the principles that you need to put in place to make sure that you can attain what it is that you want to do.

I always found it was important for me to visualize my goals. It's a powerful technique that can motivate and inspire us. You can do things like create a vision board or write down your goals. When I was younger, I participated in tap dancing and baton twirling. I knew I had to practice often in order to perform at my best. Again, breaking a goal down into small pieces to achieve it.

Understand that sometimes you schedule a time to work on a project and a challenge gets in your way. Do not get frustrated or irritated with yourself or anyone else. Just take care of whatever the challenge is and then come back to your planned schedule.

I had to learn skills to overcome obstacles. In fact, I became very adept at overcoming obstacles. I learned how to understand a problem and calm the chaos when things get out of control. It is only because I have had a lot of practice and learned how I needed to adapt.

HABITS OF SUCCESS

For most of my life, my parents exposed me to a variety of interests and experiences. They encouraged me to explore different hobbies, extracurricular activities, and subjects in school. Broadening my horizons helped me discover new passions and potential goals. It also taught me my personal skill set and what I was uniquely good at.

It's important to get the education that you need and learn life skills to overcome obstacles that come our way. The more challenges you come across the better you will be at overcoming them.

My first exposure to managing my daily time came in middle school. It was the first time of having a locker for all my books and going from classroom to classroom all over the campus. If it had not been for my 7th grade homeroom teacher teaching us time management skills, I'm not sure I would have made it. We had five minutes between classes to get to our locker and the next class. You had better be focused otherwise you would be late.

I believe that is why I am always on time in my adult life. I learned these time management skills early in life.

One thing that you learn along the way is independence and decision-making skills. I encourage you to take ownership of your goals and choices because your future is in your own hands.

It's okay to adjust your goals as circumstances change because life is unpredictable, and sometimes goals need to be adapted or modified to stay aligned with your evolving aspirations. It is important to keep supportive people around you where you can cheer each other on. Having a support network can provide valuable emotional support during challenging times.

I would encourage you to set some goals short and long-term that are empowering for you. By utilizing self-reflection, smart goal setting, and time management, you can be equipped with the skills and mindset that you are going to need to navigate your journey through life. As you grow and evolve, you'll have the tools and confidence to chase your dreams

THE PRINCIPLES OF DEBBIE & GOLIATH

and achieve your goals, contributing positively to your own life and the world around you.

"There will always be rocks in the road ahead of us. They will be stumbling blocks or steppingstones; it all depends on how you use them."

Go out and unlock your success!

SALLY WURR

About Sally Wurr: Sally Wurr is an international speaker and multi-book author.

Sally is known as the "Storm Whisperer" because her message is about how to prepare for life's storms. Each person has trials and tragedies, but it is how we react to those events that help us grow and survive in our business and personal activities.

By sharing her expertise with stories, she teaches you how to embrace change and how to face life's struggles head-on. Simply put, she likes to teach others how to problem solve.

Sally embraces the knowledge that those who can must be the ones that do. She shares her stories so that others can find their true purpose.

In addition to writing and speaking, Sally is the President and Founder of SW Insurance Corp. She has helped thousands of CEOs develop employee benefits programs to attain and retain employees. It is her problem-solving and attention to detail that have made her successful in this arena for many years.

Author's Website: *www.SallyWurr.com*
Book Series Website: *www.ThePrinciplesOfDebbieAndGoliath.com*

THE PRINCIPLES OF DEBBIE & GOLIATH

> The more I have spoken about feminism the more I have realized that fighting for women's rights has too often become synonymous with man-hating. If there is one thing I know for certain, it is that this has to stop.
>
> ~ Emma Watson

SARAH LEE

FINANCIAL LITERACY WILL SAVE THE WORLD

In the bustling city of MoneyMentorville®, there was a unique character named GPB® (Guinea Piggy Bank®). GPB® wasn't an ordinary piggy bank; he was a talking piggy bank with a cheerful personality and a shiny, golden exterior.

One day, a curious journalist named Penelope Pennywise arrived at GPB's home for an exclusive interview. GPB, with a twinkle in his eye, welcomed her in warmly. Penelope was eager to know more about GPB's life and what made him so *different*.

As they settled into a cozy corner, GPB began to share his story. "You see," he explained, "when I was young, I felt a bit different from the other piggy banks. They were content just holding coins, and teaching savings, but I always had this urge to chat and share stories and teach."

Penelope leaned in, intrigued. "That must have been hard to be so different. You are as you said, a one-of-a-kind, Guinea Piggy Bank®, different from the other "normal Piggy Banks." How did it feel to be so different?" she asked.

GPB chuckled, "Well, for starters, I could talk, and I loved to make people smile with my jokes and cheerful greetings. I have fur and I am a golden color. Plus, I giggle when someone puts a coin in me and starts to save. At times, it made me wonder if being different was a good thing."

HABITS OF SUCCESS

Penelope, sensing a deeper story, inquired more, "How did your mom and dad react to your uniqueness? Your dad is a traditional piggy bank, right? Mr. Banks and your mom a Golden Guinea, like you? It must have been a challenge at times."

GPB's eyes gleamed with warmth as he recounted, "I am now the Mayor of MoneyMentorville®, and over the years, my uniqueness has served me well. But back then, My mom and dad, wise as they are, sat me down and explained that being different is what makes me special. They said that my ability to bring joy and laughter set me apart in a wonderful way."

"They were right," GPB continued, "and as I grew older, I embraced my uniqueness. I realized that being a talking guinea piggy bank allowed me to teach the lessons of savings and financial literacy and connect with people in a way that was both magical and memorable."

Penelope smiled, capturing the essence of GPB's story. "It sounds like your parents gave you wise advice."

"They did," GPB nodded, "and now, every time someone drops a coin into my slot, it's not just about saving money. It's also about sharing a moment of joy and embracing the special quirks that make us who we are."

As the interview concluded, Penelope left with a heartwarming story of a talking guinea piggy bank who, with the love and support of his family, turned what made him different into something truly extraordinary.

This is the kind of work we do for kids at the Money Mentor® Foundation. We create stories and cartoons that are used in schools and after-school programs to help heal families and kids. With less-than-ideal financial behaviors being demonstrated in most households, Money Mentor® helps both kids and adults learn even more about money, passion, and the self-esteem needed to create success in life, both financial and literal.

THE PRINCIPLES OF DEBBIE & GOLIATH

After 20 years teaching and training adults the ins and outs of money, and as a former national investment banker and discretionary trader, with a background in education and behavioral therapy at UCLA, my husband and I, felt the need, especially during the COVID-19 pandemic, to start creating the legacy and impact that we wanted to be known for. We started to create what is now known as Money Mentor Schools, which is our afterschool program for kids to learn things that busy parents might not be able to teach their kids, often because they really do not know themselves. Money Mentor is giving adults the help and support they need whether they are homeschooling, trying to have fun or want to give their kids the best head start in life.

Teaching life skills is one of the best things we can do to set up the next generation for massive success. It is our pleasure to teach the basics of money to children at a younger age so that they:

> 1) are not afraid of money.
>
> 2) do not see money as something outside of themselves.
>
> 3) truly learn that money can be and is used to create the life of their dreams.

As humans we are constantly creating. We are constantly co-creating with God and the Universe. As the Life Force gives us ideas, we either use those ideas or those ideas get passed along to someone else who will get them out to the ones who need them and can best use them.

Working with my husband, who has spent 25 years in the professional film industry, at the likes of Disney and Lucas Films ILM, with projects like Titanic, Star Wars and Harry Potter under his belt—a multi-Academy Award Winning Special Effects film maker, (Kerry was on many teams that won the Academy Award for Visual Effects that year)—we came together to create something unique for all of the world to see. Based on the likes of a "Sesame Street-like program", that incorporates, Mindset, *Think and Grow Rich* values, financial literacy, jokes, and entertainment, we wanted to give the world something it had yet to see but desperately needs—a way to move forward.

HABITS OF SUCCESS

Giving these tools to kids, parents, and teachers alike... we hope will help to give the world the tools it needs to make a new positive and productive future. Come join us on this mission. We love you. We need you and we value you. And like all people, we want to encourage you to make your stand against poverty and stand with our kids and young ones in HOPE for a better future. Come join us! We are looking forward to meeting you soon! SFL and Klee, Founders of Money Mentor® and the Money Mentor Foundation.

Come Join the Movement!

~ Sarah Lee, Money Mentor® and MoneyMentorville®

SARAH LEE

About Sarah Lee, MBA: A brilliant educational psychologist and leadership expert by education, Sarah Lee is the innovative author of *"Rock Soup - An Innovational Idea in Leadership."* By profession, Sarah has been teaching financial literacy for the last 15 years using her own firm as a platform. She is a full-service financial advisor and manager of her own Securities Branch of a national firm. In addition, she networked with 100 Brokers all over the US. Sarah has an MBA in Finance and Social Impact and is 14 months shy of a Ph.D. in Educational Leadership. She is also the founder of multiple other companies and brands. She is now mostly currently focused on her production company with her husband, MONEY MENTOR, LLC™.

She has been advocating and speaking on large issues like financial literacy, literacy, mindset, clean water, and service to the world (hunger, water issues, poverty, and literacy) for her entire life. She is the child of a public servant. Her father was a writer (he wrote textbooks on risk and insurance practices), a city councilman in a small town who taught Sarah civic duties, service to the public, and how the national political system works. She learned how to serve others, run a nonprofit volunteer group, and make a community impact. That led to an opportunity to be "on TV (not streaming) weekly as a host" as a nine-year-old. The opportunity became more interesting when they asked Sarah what she would like to produce for Kids-4 TV. She said, "I would like to host a consumer reports show, where I would interview local business owners and see how I could highlight them while giving them ways to give back and make a difference." She was nine. That led to a life of public speaking, running endowments, and working with local universities on educational issues. She developed her world-famous business philosophy during this time: "Business is just like Rock Soup..."

Learn more about Sarah Lee, MBA, and follow her on FB: @coachmeSarahLee, @moneymentormethod; Instagram: @moneymentorcompany, @coachmeacademy. For Money Tips, you can text the words "MONEYMENTOR" to 55444 for a free gift or visit our webpage: linktr.ee/MoneyMentorMethod.

Author's Website: *www.MoneyMentorFreeGift.com*

Book Series Website: *www.ThePrinciplesOfDebbieAndGoliath.com*

STEPH SHINABERY
FINDING MY VOICE & STRENGTH

A Tower of Strength

Growing up taller than most of my peers, including boys, was a mixed blessing. It set me apart in sports, giving me an edge, but it also made me painfully self-conscious. I remember the stares, the whispered comments, and the feeling of being an outsider. It took years to realize that my height was not a liability but a unique asset, something that made me stand out for all the right reasons. I learned to carry my height with pride, transforming from a self-conscious teen to a confident woman who could walk into any room and command respect.

From the early days of towering over classmates on the playground to navigating the complex terrain of adult life, my journey has been one of constant evolution, challenge, and self-discovery. This chapter is more than just my story; it's a reflection of the battles fought and won, both on the sports field and within myself.

Growing up, I was always the tallest kid in my class. It was a defining characteristic that set me apart from my peers, but it also came with its own set of challenges. I struggled to find clothes that fit properly, and I often felt awkward and clumsy. But as I got older, I began to embrace my height and appreciate the unique perspective it gave me.

As a teenager, I discovered a passion for sports. Basketball, in particular, became my outlet for self-expression and competition. I loved the feeling of pushing my body to its limits and the sense of camaraderie that came from playing on a team. But sports also taught me some difficult lessons about perseverance, resilience, and the importance of hard work.

As I entered adulthood, I faced new challenges and struggles. I had to navigate the complexities of relationships, career choices, and personal growth. But through it all, I learned to lean into my strengths and face my weaknesses head-on. This chapter of my story is a testament to the power of resilience, determination, and self-discovery.

The Battle for Inclusion in Sports

The battle to play sports as a girl wasn't just about the physical act of playing; it was about breaking barriers and challenging norms. Each rejection from a boys' team wasn't merely a 'no' to participation; it was a denial of my potential. I remember the mixed feelings of triumph and isolation when I'd outperform the boys in impromptu basketball games. It was a bittersweet victory, proving my worth yet being denied official recognition. These experiences were my early lessons in resilience and perseverance, qualities that have been my companions ever since.

I recall my teenage years with a mix of emotions. Standing 5'10" and weighing 120 pounds, I was an awkward presence among my peers. It was during this time that my love for sports collided with societal norms. I yearned to play football, to be part of a team, but was constantly reminded that 'girls don't play football.' This exclusion wasn't just about the game; it was a statement about where girls supposedly belonged.

But I refused to be sidelined. I remember trying to join the boys' basketball team in fifth grade, only to be turned away. This rejection fueled a fire within me, a determination that said, "Watch me prove you wrong." I practiced relentlessly, often alone, driven by a mix of passion and anger. Looking back, I see that while this drive was empowering, it also masked an underlying frustration, a sense of injustice that I couldn't articulate then.

My perseverance ultimately paid off. That experience taught me the power of pushing past rejection and using it as a catalyst for growth. It also made me aware of the gender biases that existed in sports and other areas of life. As I grew older, I became more vocal about advocating for gender equality and other social issues. But I never forgot that initial rejection and the fire it ignited in me. It taught me that sometimes the greatest motivation comes from being told "no."

Advice to My Younger Self

If I could speak to my 13-year-old self, I'd tell her that there's always a path forward. I would tell her that life is full of challenges, but each challenge is an opportunity to learn and grow. There will be times when things seem impossible, but it's important to remember that those are just moments, and they will pass. I would encourage her to always believe in herself, even when others doubt her. To be confident, but also humble. To work hard, but also give herself time to rest and recharge. And most importantly, to never give up on her dreams, no matter how big or small they may be. Because with hard work, determination, and a positive attitude, anything is possible.

Instead of fighting back with raw might, the key is to seek guidance, to find allies and mentors. Back then, women in sports were rare, and advocating for our place was a lonely battle. But I've learned that it's crucial to voice your dreams and find those who will listen and help pave the way.

A Journey of Self-Discovery

My exploration into empowerment was not a sudden epiphany but a gradual awakening. It started with a curiosity about the deeper aspects of relationships, leading me to books, workshops, and eventually, a certification program. This path has been about more than internal exploration; it's been a journey into the depths of emotional and spiritual connection, understanding the power of vulnerability and trust.

Through this journey, I have learned that true empowerment comes from a combination of self-awareness, self-love, and a willingness to be vulnerable. It's about recognizing our own strengths and limitations, and accepting and embracing all parts of ourselves, even the parts that we may not be proud of. It's about standing in our power and owning our worth, while also being open to learning, growing, and evolving.

Empowerment also involves recognizing the power dynamics at play in our relationships and society as a whole. It's about challenging the status quo and advocating for ourselves and others. It's about creating space for diverse voices and perspectives to be heard and valued. And it's about lifting others up as we rise, rather than tearing them down.

Ultimately, empowerment is a journey that requires ongoing commitment and effort. It's not always easy, but it's worth it. As we become more empowered, we are able to create positive change in our own lives and in the world around us.

The Struggle with Self-Expression

As I grew older, the battlefields changed, but the fight remained similar. I've always grappled with self-expression, often editing myself based on others' expectations or beliefs. This pattern followed me into adulthood, influencing my career choices and personal life.

A poignant example is my journey with sexuality and relationships. Coming out was a monumental step for me, one that required peeling back layers of conditioned beliefs and fears. It was about more than revealing my truth; it was about accepting and loving myself fully.

Navigating relationships as a queer person can be challenging, especially when societal norms and expectations are often built around a heteronormative framework. But I've come to realize that embracing my identity and being true to myself is the most important thing. It's allowed me to form deeper connections with others who share similar experiences and values. And while there may still be obstacles to overcome, I'm grateful for the progress that's been made and the community that's been built. I hope that one day, everyone can feel empowered to embrace their authentic selves and love without fear or shame.

THE PRINCIPLES OF DEBBIE & GOLIATH

The Challenge of Self-Expression in Professional Spaces

Navigating self-expression in professional spaces has been a complex dance. Working in environments that often don't encourage open discussions about sexuality and personal beliefs has been challenging. I've had to learn the art of balancing my personal convictions with professional decorum, understanding when to speak and when to listen. This journey has been about finding my voice in spaces that aren't always receptive, and learning to express myself in ways that are authentic yet respectful of the diversity of opinions and beliefs in the workplace.

It's not always easy to find the right balance between self-expression and professionalism. On one hand, it's important to be true to ourselves and to speak up about issues that matter to us. On the other hand, we need to be mindful of the fact that we are in a professional setting, where different people have different perspectives and opinions.

One thing that has helped me navigate this complex terrain is to be clear about my own values and beliefs, and to understand how they relate to my work. This has allowed me to find common ground with colleagues who may have different views, and to engage in constructive conversations about issues that matter to us.

Another strategy that has worked well for me is to listen more than I speak. By taking the time to really hear what others are saying, I can better understand their perspectives and find ways to work together towards common goals. This has helped me build strong relationships with colleagues and to create a more inclusive and welcoming workplace culture.

Ultimately, navigating self-expression in professional spaces is about finding a way to be true to ourselves while also being respectful of others. It's not always easy, but with practice and patience, we can learn to find our voice and to make a positive impact in our workplaces and beyond.

Confronting Family Dynamics

My journey of self-acceptance and expression was further complicated by family dynamics. Coming out was a monumental step, but it was just the beginning of a longer journey of navigating my relationships with family members who had different views and values. It was a delicate balance of staying true to myself while trying to maintain familial bonds. These experiences taught me the importance of setting boundaries and the power of compassionate communication.

Through this journey, I have also come to appreciate the importance of finding a supportive community. Having a group of people who understand and accept you for who you are can make all the difference in the world. It can be challenging to find this community, but it is worth the effort. Whether it's through LGBTQ+ groups, online forums, or close friends, it's crucial to have a support system to turn to during difficult times.

Ultimately, I have learned that self-acceptance and expression are ongoing processes. It's not something that happens overnight, and it's not always easy. But the journey is worth it. Embracing who you are and living authentically can lead to a fulfilling and rewarding life. It's a journey that requires patience, self-compassion, and a willingness to be vulnerable and courageous. I hope that my experiences can inspire others to embark on their own journey of self-discovery and acceptance.

The Power of Authenticity and Finding Your Tribe

Through these experiences, I've learned the importance of authenticity and surrounding myself with the right people. Your tribe, those who understand and support you, are invaluable. They are the ones who help protect that fragile flame of self-belief as you navigate the complexities of self-expression.

Being authentic means being true to yourself and your values, without trying to conform to the expectations of others. It can be scary to show the world who you really are, but the freedom and fulfillment that comes with it is worth it.

Finding your tribe is also crucial. These are the people who will lift you up when you're feeling down, celebrate your successes, and offer a listening ear when you need it. They will also challenge you to grow and improve, both personally and professionally.

Surrounding yourself with the right people can make all the difference in achieving your goals and living a happy life. So, take the time to find your tribe and be your authentic self. You'll be amazed at the positive impact it can have on your life.

But finding your tribe isn't always easy, especially when it means distancing yourself from those who don't understand or accept your truth. I've had to make tough choices, like limiting my exposure to certain family members on social media, to maintain my authenticity.

The Launch of My Coaching Business

Launching my coaching business felt like stepping off a cliff into the unknown. It was a culmination of my experiences, learnings, and a desire to empower others. This venture is not just about imparting knowledge; it's about creating a space where people can explore, learn, and grow in their personal journeys. My aim is to offer guidance and support, helping others navigate their paths with more ease and confidence than I had at their stage.

Starting a business can be daunting, particularly when it's something you're passionate about. It can feel like a huge risk to put your heart and soul into something and then put it out into the world for others to judge. But for me, the potential rewards far outweighed the risks. I knew that if I could create a business that truly helped people, it would be worth all the hard work and uncertainty.

As I worked to establish my coaching business, I focused on building a strong foundation of knowledge and skills. I quickly realized that the most important thing I could offer my clients was not just expertise, but empathy.

HABITS OF SUCCESS

Everyone's journey is different, and what works for one person may not work for another. That's why I strive to create a space where each client feels heard, understood, and supported. I work with them to identify their unique strengths and challenges, and to create a plan that is tailored to their individual needs.

Of course, there are still moments when I feel unsure or overwhelmed. But I remind myself that this is all part of the journey. And when I see the progress my clients make, when I witness the lightbulb moments and the breakthroughs, I know that I'm exactly where I'm meant to be.

Embarking on New Ventures

Now, as I venture into the world of coaching, focusing on areas like tantra and sexual empowerment, I am again at a crossroads. Starting this business feels like stepping into uncharted territory, where my personal beliefs and professional aspirations intersect in unfamiliar ways. It's a journey of not only guiding others but also continually learning and evolving myself.

Looking back on my journey, I see a tapestry of triumphs, setbacks, and growth. Each experience, whether joyful or painful, has contributed to my understanding of empowerment. Looking forward, my goal is to continue evolving, both personally and professionally, and to use my voice and experiences to inspire and uplift others. I am committed to being a beacon of hope and strength for those who are finding their way through similar struggles.

Reflections and Looking Forward

As I prepare for new experiences, I am reminded of the importance of pacing oneself. Life is a marathon, not a sprint. The lessons learned, and the battles fought, all contribute to who I am today and who we all become. It's a time to celebrate the victories, acknowledge the struggles, and look forward to the future with optimism and an open heart.

My story is still being written, with each day bringing new challenges and opportunities for growth. Through it all, I've learned that our greatest strength lies in our authenticity and our willingness to embrace our unique paths. I hope that by sharing my story, I can encourage others to embrace their uniqueness, to find their strength, and to live their truth with confidence and pride.

STEPH SHINABERY

About Steph Shinabery: Steph Shinabery is The World's Best Possibility Coach, and a Nurse Anesthesiologist, Artist, Speaker, and the Founder of GENIUS CODE ACADEMY.

After spending much of her life in a career that lacked the inspiration and fulfillment she knew was available to her, she began a journey to answer the question: "What is it I truly desire?"

Her journey led to the creation of the Genius Identity Code™, a process for unlocking your gift, purpose and path, and helping people see, believe and execute their unique genius to achieve miraculous outcomes.

Steph works with creative experts, entrepreneurs and coaches to help them embrace their authenticity and create a life that gets them excited to jump out of bed every day!

You can find her talk, "Wake Up Your Genius Machine" on Amazon Prime Video's Speak Up: Empower Your Ideas, Season 4.

Author's Website: *www.StephShinabery.com* & *www.GeniusCodeAcademy.com*

Book Series Website: *www.ThePrinciplesOfDebbieAndGoliath.com*

TAMMY THACKER

BREAKING BOUNDARIES: FROM LAW ENFORCEMENT TO ENTREPRENEURSHIP

Growing up, I was incredibly blessed with two amazing parents. My upbringing was unconventional in the best possible way. Traditional gender roles did not define our family dynamic. My parents were deeply involved in our day-to-day lives. He did laundry, cooked, and cared for us just as much as my mom did. My siblings and I were treated as a team, with no tasks explicitly designated for boys or girls. This egalitarian approach significantly impacted me, shaping my belief that I could do anything, regardless of my gender.

I played sports throughout my childhood—basketball, volleyball, and softball. I loved being active and spent a lot of time outdoors, hiking, fishing, and snowmobiling. My parents never catered to stereotypes. My sister and I were expected to help build sheds and work in the yard, just as my brothers were expected to help with cooking and laundry. This upbringing instilled in me a sense of independence and a belief that I could achieve anything I set my mind to.

One of the most memorable lessons from my dad occurred after a particularly tough basketball game. I was upset, complaining about the referees and how unfairly I had been treated. My dad stopped me and said, "I didn't see that. What I saw was the girl you were up against giving 120%, and you gave 100." He taught me that I couldn't control external factors like referees or opponents but could control my effort and attitude. This lesson of taking responsibility for my own actions and striving to be the best I could be has stayed with me throughout my life.

Choosing a Path: From EMT to Law Enforcement

Initially, I wanted to go into sports medicine. When I was 19, I took an EMT class and became an EMT. During this class, I met several law enforcement officers and was captivated by their stories. I realized that being a police officer was what I needed to do. I had to wait until I was 21 to become an officer, so I continued working as an EMT, loving the medical field.

My journey to becoming a police officer wasn't straightforward. I got married and had a son, and the dream of law enforcement stayed with me. When I was 26, I got my corrections certification. Later, at 32, I went through the second block of training to obtain my LEO Certification. This was challenging—I was older, not in the best shape, and balancing full-time work and motherhood. But I persevered, attending night school and weekend classes until I graduated.

I started my career in law enforcement in Heber City, where I was hired and sponsored to complete my training. It wasn't easy, but I had an incredible support system within, not only my little family but my amazing parents.

The Challenges of a Female Officer

Being a female in a male-dominated field was tough. There were those who trusted me and those who didn't, some of whom I could win over and some I couldn't. I had to dig deep to prove myself, leaning heavily on my faith. Each shift began with a prayer, asking for strength and guidance.

One of the most challenging aspects of my job was the responsibility that came with it. For 15 of my 20 years in law enforcement, I worked in investigations, making decisions that significantly impacted people's lives. Arresting someone for a crime like sexual assault might mean turning their family's world upside down. While necessary, these actions weighed heavily on me, and I often leaned on my higher power to help me make the right decisions and provide the support needed for those affected.

Overcoming Personal Doubts

One of my biggest challenges has been believing in myself throughout my life. Despite my accomplishments, I often struggled with self-doubt. I faced many naysayers who didn't want to see me succeed, especially in a male-dominated field. But I learned to get out of my own way, be humble, and recognize that I was often my biggest obstacle.

Even now, I sometimes fake confidence until I truly feel it. This is a common experience for many people. The external world can be harsh, constantly chipping away at your self-esteem. But through it all, I've learned to hold my head high and push through.

A New Chapter: Entrepreneurship

At 46, I retired from law enforcement and transitioned into entrepreneurship. My best friend, Amy Madsen, and with the support of Team Karl Malone were able to start our new adventure. We were approached by Black Rifle Coffee, a company that supports the military and first responders—values that resonated deeply with me. One of the things I loved most about being in law enforcement was the service aspect. I felt fulfilled when serving others, and I saw this business as an extension of that service.

Amy, who shares my passion for supporting the military and first responders, and I decided to open a Black Rifle Coffee franchise. My husband still had several years to work before he could retire, and I knew I couldn't sit idle. I thrive when busy and felt this venture was the perfect fit.

HABITS OF SUCCESS

Serving the Community

My children have always been involved in community service; a value instilled in them from birth. Both my children inspire me to be a better person every day.

Service has always been a cornerstone of my life. Whether through law enforcement or business, helping others gives me a sense of purpose and fulfillment. When life gets tough, I look for ways to serve, knowing it will lift my spirits and make a difference in someone else's life.

Lessons Learned and Advice for the Future

Reflecting on my journey, I would tell my younger self to believe in herself and have confidence. Growing up, I struggled with insecurity and was bullied in high school. But I found strength in my support system and learned to trust myself. My advice to my 13-year-old self and anyone reading this is to trust your heart, ignore the naysayers, and be confident in who you are. You are perfect just the way you are.

Having these challenges did not stop me—I became the first female detective and the first female sergeant for Heber City Police. One of my favorite quotes or sayings is, "It's not my business what people say about me." I try daily to live by this and not worry about things or people I have no control over.

The Importance of Support

I was fortunate to have a supportive family. My parents were amazing role models; my husband and children have been my rock. Their belief in me gave me the strength to overcome my challenges. My mom and dad taught me the importance of serving others and being compassionate, values I've passed on to my children.

Transitioning from law enforcement to entrepreneurship has been a rewarding journey. It's allowed me to continue serving my community in a new way. Black Rifle Coffee's mission aligns perfectly with my values, supporting the military and first responders and providing a space for community and connection.

My story is one of perseverance, faith, and service. I've faced many challenges, but each one has made me stronger. I've learned that believing in yourself, having a strong support system, and serving others is key to overcoming any obstacle. Whether in law enforcement or business, my goal has always been to impact others' lives positively. As I continue this journey, I'm grateful for the lessons learned and the people who have supported me along the way.

In the end, we all have our Goliaths to face. How we confront them with courage, faith, and a commitment to service defines our success. Believe in yourself, trust your journey, and never underestimate the power of serving others.

TAMMY THACKER

About Tammy Thacker: Tammy Thacker, a distinguished figure in Heber City, Utah, epitomizes the blend of dedication to public service and entrepreneurial spirit. Raised in Heber City, Tammy's journey began at Wasatch High School, where she laid the foundations of her commitment to her community.

Tammy's career in law enforcement, marked by tenures at both the Heber City Police Department and the Wasatch County Sheriff's Office, reflects her unwavering commitment to public safety and community wellbeing. Her time in local law enforcement not only allowed her to serve her community but also provided her with invaluable experiences that shaped her leadership and organizational skills.

Transitioning from law enforcement to the business world, Tammy embarked on a new venture as the leader of Black Rifle Coffee Company in Heber City. This entrepreneurial leap showcases her versatile skill set and her ability to adapt and thrive in diverse environments. At Black Rifle Coffee Roasters, she combines her deep understanding of the local community with her leadership abilities, steering the company towards growth while maintaining its core values.

Amidst her professional endeavors, Tammy remains deeply rooted in her community and family life in Heber City. Her story is a testament to her resilience, adaptability, and enduring commitment to her hometown.

Author's Website: www.BlackRifleCoffee.com

Book Series Website: www.ThePrinciplesOfDebbieAndGoliath.com

TASHA SMITH
FROM ME TO YOU

"This is dedicated to my beautiful princesses. Always remember that the sky is your only limit. Your capabilities are endless if you continue to keep dreaming!"
~ Love Always, Mom

When I was a little girl, the world looked so colorful in my eyes. Before I woke up in the morning, I had dreamed about what I would do for the day. I dreamt about playing with my friends, dressing my dolls, riding my bike, looking for rainbows, and chasing butterflies under the bright sunny skies.

As I got a little older, now in double digits, the world started to look a little different to me. It was still colorful but now the colors had changed from pastels to more primary colors. In my eyes, the world was changing. The reality was that it was me that was changing. I was growing up. My interests were different, I had new friends, and the way that I went about my life had all changed. Then I became a teenager!

No one had warned me of this major development. My thoughts, body, and views were now different. Also, there was something else that changed. Now, there was this thing called "expectations" that the world had of me. This was something that I did not like. It felt as if all eyes were on me, like someone was using a magnifying glass with a highlighter to zero in on every little detail of me.

HABITS OF SUCCESS

I think I was a normal teen depending on what your version of normal is. I was by no means perfect, but overall, I was a good kid. Over time things started to get a bit difficult for me. This is where you should listen closely and take notes...

Then, I was in high school and I had to start making major decisions for myself. This was something new for me because most of the decisions that were made in my life were made by my parents. Making decisions for myself was not the difficult part. Making decisions that they agreed with was the difficult part. I had to be smart enough to make the right choice and at the same time try and figure out how to persuade them to accept my decisions and not kick them back.

My household consisted of two headstrong parents. If they did not agree they would let you know, immediately, so that you could change your stance. Unfortunately for them, I am a combination of them both. Fortunately for myself, I possess their headstrong qualities along with my own personality traits. So, with all that being said, we bumped heads on the regular. I like to call it growing pains. When we are born, we do not come with a set of instructions. Our parents try and do their best as they go along. The same goes for kids, we also figure it out as we go along with our parents.

For me, I had to figure out that they meant well but my choices would not always coincide with theirs. I wish I had a looking glass that could have taught me how to please them and make myself happy at the same time. Luckily for you, I am here to let you know that it is okay to go after what you are passionate about, even at an early age. Our parents mean well but at the same time your dreams and passions should not be stifled or discouraged because they do not see your vision.

If there is something that you are truly interested in, it is your duty to yourself to pursue it and try. If you do not, you could possibly walk around with regret and that is something that you should never have.

Dreams are something that we all have. They are like noses; we all have them, but they are all different. When pursuing your dreams, you must put in the time and hard work to see them come to fruition. Also, do not

THE PRINCIPLES OF DEBBIE & GOLIATH

be afraid to ask for help. Often when your family or community notices the dedication and hard work that you are committing to your dreams, they may become willing to assist you in accomplishing your goal.

Once you have reached your goal of accomplishing your dreams you now have the task of deciding who will remain in your circle. When I was a younger woman in my late twenties or early thirties, life was taking me on some roller coaster rides around the world. During that time, one of my uncles became aware of the amusement park journey that I was on, so he composed a poem and sent it to me.

In this poem, he explained to me that life was like a theater stage production. In this production, we are the actors on stage and the audience members are the people in our life. In this production of my life, I got to decide where the audience members would sit. My biggest supporters and favorite people sat front and center. The people that I loved but were not good for my life were seated on the balcony. The toxic people were seated all the way in the back of the theater in nosebleed seats.

While you are on your journey to accomplishing your dreams, you may encounter many of the people who may appear to be in your corner. Some of the people may be genuinely proud of and happy for you and others may not. So, you must be very selective with your production and the placement of your audience members' seating.

You may be very young right now reading this, so what I am saying may seem very humorous. The purpose of this sharing is to teach you early on to be mindful of who you let into your life. Sometimes we get so caught up with having fun and living our best life that we let any and everybody in it. By the time we realize what is going on and who is doing what, it is too late, and feelings are hurt. That is why it is important to surround yourself with good people who are always, no matter what, members of team YOU!

Allow me to be a personal life guide with this simple, yet profound counsel. If I had someone to foresee and guide me through life, I would have made many different choices to accomplish larger goals. Not to say that I made bad or horrible decisions in my life, I would have just made more appropriate ones. However, I do not have many major regrets at this stage in my life. With life comes gained experience, or wisdom, and sometimes even patience. Even though I am still a work in progress, I have come to somewhat appreciate my life journey thus far. Because of all the adventures that life has taken me on, it has molded me into the person that I am today and I know it will do the same for you too.

I think you will be pleased with the person that you turn out to be. You have accomplished several things in life. To date, I think my most impressive accomplishment was deciding to become a mother—a mom to four beautiful, smart, talented, and highly intelligent individuals who are genuinely kind people. They turned out extremely well!

TASHA SMITH

About Tasha Smith: Tasha is a resident of North Carolina by way of New York. She is a mom of four and loves spending quality time with her family. In her spare time, Tasha creates various DIY crafts and interior design projects. Her favorite kind of entertainment is attending concerts, plays, and comedy shows. In the future, one of Tasha's greatest aspirations is to help provide shelter and assistance to those who are in need and less fortunate.

Book Series Website: *www.ThePrinciplesOfDebbieAndGoliath.com*

HABITS OF SUCCESS

TAYLOR L. COLE
CONFIDENTLY LEVELING UP

Tucked away in the back of a spare closet lies a tattered purple duffle bag, its velcro handles showing signs of age. To the eye, it's nothing particularly remarkable. There's no convenient phone charging cable or a pocket to securely hold water. It doesn't even have a luggage tag attached. Yet, within its frayed seams and faded fabric resides a trove of memories, marking a pivotal chapter from my adolescence when I was on the brink of my blissful tweens.

Do you remember that feeling as a kid when there was this one thing you really wanted? Maybe you saved up your allowance or did extra chores to earn the money. You spotted it in a store, online, or in a magazine, and you just knew you had to have it. After all that saving and hard work, you finally got your hands on that cherished item! That was me in my tweens.

Back then, I knew everything I was going to pack into the purple duffle bag. I was a middle school cheerleader living on a beautiful ranch nestled in a quaint town in Oklahoma. My close-knit community consisted of both sets of grandparents, my amazing parents, aunts, uncles, cousins, and friends. In my mind, I had everything I believed I needed or desired. A sizable residence surrounded by an extensive property with barns, stables, pastures, gardens, and a menagerie of livestock—cattle, ducks, chickens, hogs, along with a variety of dogs and cats.

My grandma Mamma Fannie was a strong woman of God who radiated with Godly confidence. She taught me to reach up, to seek God first in everything I did. She'd often quote:

HABITS OF SUCCESS

"I am convinced and confident of this very thing, that He who began a good work in you will continue to perfect it and complete it until the day of Christ Jesus."
~ Philippians 1:6

She taught me that if I'd reach up to God, I'd always find the Godly confidence I needed to get through any situation. Little did I know that I'd need that advice much sooner than I'd ever anticipated.

There was a day that almost felt like perfection. We started with breakfast together—Daddy, Mom, and I—listening to our favorite music, laughing, dancing, and sharing hugs. In the afternoon, Mom and I took a long walk, singing songs and just reveling in the joy of each other's company. During that time, so much in my life felt certain and secure.

So, it came as a complete shock to me when, at the age of 12, late that same night, my mom burst into my room, woke me abruptly, and instructed me to pack up everything I could. "What?" I was in disbelief! I was half asleep, but I asked her to say it again because I must have heard her incorrectly. But sadly, I hadn't been mistaken. Mommy said, "Get up. Pack everything you can because we're leaving this house, and I don't think we'll ever be able to return again!" I was heartbroken. We were leaving behind not just our home, town, and extended family, but also everything I'd ever known. With tear-filled eyes, I grabbed my purple duffle bag, filled it to the brim with my belongings then grabbed everything my little arms could carry. I slowly glanced back at my framed photos, dolls, video games, those schoolbooks that I kept long after I'd completed the book report, and so many beautiful memories.

In an instant, all my dreams and my plans were gone, and I felt steamrolled. I was derailed. Have you ever felt like the rug was pulled right from under you? Have you ever had what you thought to be solid plans and hopes for the future, and it suddenly vanishes? That night, we went to a family member's house, and we barely got settled before we had to leave again and go to the YWCA, and the next thing I knew we were in a battered women's shelter. I would come to realize that in spite of how much my parents showed undying love for me, their marriage had lots of problems and my mom was the victim of domestic violence. I

THE PRINCIPLES OF DEBBIE & GOLIATH

was angry! Angry at my Daddy. Disappointed in my mom. Angry that the life I loved was no more.

We left luxury and comfort for confusion and chaos. I spent many tear-filled nights lonely and afraid. Often the only things I could carry would fit in my purple duffle bag. Yet, my mom had to stand up to protect me and herself. Once I got over looking at the situation from my own perspective, I got the courage to have a long talk with my mom. I wanted to understand how she found the courage to stand up and make that difficult choice, on that day. My mom told me a story of her mother and an example she learned from her.

My grandmother Alma on my mom's side of the family was a gifted writer. Her dream was to be a reporter at a large newspaper and share the news of her town with an even bigger community. One day she gathered her carefully crafted articles and walked into the office at the newspaper publisher in the county. She felt good about her work and was looking forward to getting a job. But the newspaper publisher told her that although she was a good writer, he couldn't accept stories from a woman like her. He said that a Native American and black woman in her day in this town wouldn't be allowed to write for the white-owned newspaper. She went back home and decided she'd show up anyway. She created her own newsletter, manually printed copies with carbon paper, and shared the news of her community throughout the entire area. She wrote stories of births, new businesses, successes, celebrations, and loved ones lost. She had such a big following (and this was long before Instagram!) that people started sending her their stories and financial contributions to make sure she could keep the news coming. Finally, the publisher for the main paper in town, that very one that turned her down years before, invited her to come into his office for a meeting. Not only did he ask her to write for the newspaper, but he gave her a column of her own, told her she could feature any news she wanted, and told her he already had advertisers lined up to support her work.

My grandma had the Godly confidence in who she was, and in her abilities and she chose to show up for her community even in the face of rejection. In her fifties, she achieved a significant milestone, becoming the first woman of color to serve as a columnist in our county. She amplified the stories of families and communities that otherwise didn't have a channel to share their voices. Her determination to represent and advocate for those unheard was truly remarkable. My grandmother chose to show up.

Meanwhile, my parents' marriage ended after taking several years for the divorce to be finalized. I harbored resentment and struggled immensely to let go of the past, clinging to my shattered dreams of what I believed should have been. I was still heartbroken, and I had lots of questions for my Daddy. Why would he and how could he hurt my mom? How was it that he was raised in a loving home with Godly examples, yet he made such bad choices. One day, he and I had a long, difficult conversation and asked him why. My Daddy shared with me that the divorce taught him a significant lesson. He emphasized that apart from seeking forgiveness and repentance, a crucial aspect was his need to mature and grow up. He said he had to grow up and grow into the man that God had designed him to be. He said even in his forties at the time, he had to grow up and recognize his mistakes but not let those mistakes define him. He had confidence that the mistakes in his past, wouldn't define him. Confidence comes from not always being right, but from not fearing being wrong. It was his growth mindset and Godly confidence that helped him through.

It's truly a blessing to have been shaped and guided by the lessons from three remarkable women and one loving, humble man. Their wisdom and influence have directed me towards embracing Godly confidence in my life. Reach up, stand up, show up, grow up. I learned that confidence isn't something you put in a bag, but it's in you. It's through Christ who began a good work in you.

Reach Up: Did you know that you can remain confident in the fact that He who began a good work in you will be faithful to complete it until the day of Christ Jesus? That you have access to Godly confidence? That no matter what you're facing, God can see in you what no one else can see.

Stand Up: Where do you need to take a stand? What injustices, what hurts and what wrongs are you seeing that you need to stand up to? Where can you take a stand?

Show Up: Who is going unseen? Who has faded into obscurity because they don't have an advocate? Where can you show up? Where can your presence make a difference with just your being there and present?

Grow Up: How can we all grow into our purpose and become everything we've been destined to become?
This might require you to speak up, to be an active voice for someone to encourage them, or for a cause without a champion. Even through hardships, we can reach up, stand up, show up, grow up, and speak up. What's your next step? Are you ready to confidently level up?

TLC

TAYLOR L. COLE

About Taylor L. Cole: Taylor L. Cole is a seasoned professional dedicated to helping meaningful brands capture the attention they deserve. With a career spanning over 14 years, Taylor has honed her skills in Communications, PR, and social media, working with Fortune 500 companies, multi-national corporations, and startups across various industries including travel, tech, healthcare, and consumer products.

Starting her journey in the world of television while still in high school, Taylor quickly made her mark, producing her first major show as an undergraduate at Southern Methodist University. She has since taken on leadership roles in communications and public relations at renowned companies such as Kimberly Clark, Hotels.com, Expedia, and Sabre.

Taylor's extensive experience has allowed her to work with a diverse range of business owners, entertainers, and travel suppliers, teaching her the crucial lesson that brands must captivate their audience with the right marketing exposure to avoid falling into obscurity.

As a guide for brands and leaders, Taylor specializes in crafting effective messaging and on-camera strategies, featuring her clients on quality, international TV programs and podcasts. She is the executive producer and host of "The Focus" and "Speak Up" on Amazon Prime Video, as well as the travel TV show "Hotel Hunt," where she explores stunning destinations and uncovers unique accommodations. Her latest project is "Workable Faith," a show where she engages with business leaders about integrating faith into the marketplace. Taylor is also a dedicated community member, serving on various non-profit boards, business leadership groups, and actively participating in her church. Her involvement includes roles with the American Diabetes Association, Fellowship Power Lunch, Truth at Work, Valley Creek Church, and SMU.

She invites brands ready to step into the spotlight to connect with her at TVwithTLC.com, where they can embark on a journey to refine their messaging, identify their key audience, and build the perfect platform to share their unique voice. Taylor's specialties encompass a wide range of services including being a Brand Spokesperson, TV Host for Travel & Lifestyle Products, TV Production, Podcasting, Christian Businesses and Values-Based Initiatives, Author & Professional Speaker Visibility, Strategic Public Relations, Marketing Consulting, Communications Strategy, Media Coaching & Training, and serving as a Fractional Communications & PR Executive. She is the proven fixer that brands need to shine in their respective industries.

Author's Website: *www.TVWithTLC.com*

Book Series Website: *www.ThePrinciplesOfDebbieAndGoliath.com*

HABITS OF SUCCESS

THE PRINCIPLES OF DEBBIE & GOLIATH

> Justice is about making sure that being polite is not the same thing as being quiet. In fact, often times, the most righteous thing you can do is shake the table.

~ Alexandria Ocasio-Cortez

HABITS OF SUCCESS

VIKKI ROOD

FROM JUNIOR HIGH BLUES TO ETSY HUES: A STORY OF RESILIENCE

Ah, the delightful drama of junior high, where the world was as stable as a roller coaster on steroids. Every day felt like navigating a maze where I had to pretend I fit in. I mastered the art of saying just enough to blend in and not enough to stand out.

Why? Well, I sported a chip on my shoulder, thanks to the hand-me-downs that adorned my less-than-luxurious wardrobe. While my pals were packing for the 8th-grade escapade to D.C., I was mastering the fine art of latchkey babysitting. Unfair? You bet. FOMO? It practically wrote the story of my teenage angst.

And let's talk fashion. High hair, Aqua Net, and the belief that my worth was as good as my latest hairstyle. Hand-me-downs? Oh, I turned them into a fashion statement. I was a comparison ninja, always sizing up against others. Outwardly happy, inwardly insecure—the classic junior high paradox.

But hey, here's the golden nugget I stumbled upon: everyone's got their bag of self-doubt. Turns out, we were all in the comparison game, just passing around spiral notebooks instead of Instagram likes. Theodore Roosevelt had it right: "Comparison is the thief of joy."

HABITS OF SUCCESS

In this pre-social media era, imperfections were like rare gems. Life, by default, is a wild ride of uncertainty. Instead of bemoaning it, I've learned to dance with the chaos. Uncertainty? It's not a roadblock; it's the scenic route, full of opportunities, possibilities, and adventures that forge badass skills.

So, here's to the messy, the imperfect, and the gloriously uncertain—where our sparks truly shine. Life's a roller coaster, darling. Might as well throw your hands up and enjoy the ride.

Ah, the pursuit of being the poster child for "good," "nice," and "likable." I once embarked on the noble quest for lifeguard certification, convinced that the judgmental eyes of the universe were locked onto me. Picture this: waiting to save a lifeguard, and of course, it had to be the one I had a crush on. The plot thickens.

Enter the swim team philosopher, who, with a touch of my face and a gaze into my eyes, dropped a truth bomb: "Vikki, screw what everyone thinks. Just let it go. All that matters is you give it your best shot. Fate will do the rest." Sixteen-year-old wisdom that I've clung to ever since. It's a mantra: me against me, the eternal battle.

Conforming, my dear, is the extinguisher of your spark, the muzzler of your gifts, the serial killer of your authenticity. Recently, I stumbled upon an analogy that sheds light on my emotional horsepower. Picture this: you're either a Prius, the slow and steady emotional cruiser, or a Porsche, emotions going from 0 to 60 in seconds. Guess which one I am? Yep, the emotional Ferrari.

Sure, it might be what holds me back at times, but it's also the secret sauce for the wonder and awe in my life. Holding back means missing out on a front-row seat to my own spectacular emotional fireworks. When you stifle that inner self, it's like trying to cork up a volcano. Spoiler alert: it blows, and it's messy. Turns out, my sensitive, emotional rollercoaster isn't a flaw; it's a VIP pass to a broader spectrum of understanding. So, here's to letting the emotional Porsche roar and enjoying the chaos it brings. Life's too short for emotional speed limits, don't you think?

THE PRINCIPLES OF DEBBIE & GOLIATH

Ah, the spark within you—it's like a mystical unicorn, dazzling and a bit elusive, even to the proud unicorn owner (that's you). Most folks won't get it, but who cares? Your magnificence isn't for the faint-hearted—it's magnetic, baby. Your love for life spills over like an overfilled cup at a never-ending brunch, touching everyone around you.

Now, in the grand circus of confusion, remember this: the wonder and awe of the world don't need a GPS. Embrace the nonsensical; that's where your magic resides. Forget playing it safe; sing like you're auditioning for Broadway, tell stories like a bard, and gaze at stars like they owe you money. Life's beauty isn't found in the cozy corners; it's in the risks taken and the stories lived out loud.

Sure, hiding your magic might seem like an easier game of hide-and-seek, but guess what? It always resurfaces. So, when that spark tingles your insides, don't be a magician's assistant; acknowledge it. Write about it, shout it from the metaphorical rooftops. You'll align with the universe, and suddenly, everything clicks like a cosmic Rubik's Cube.

Now, my journey wasn't a seamless stroll down a glittery runway. I've danced with doubt, waltzed with embarrassment, and had a full-blown tango with heartbreak. But you know what? It sculpted me into this proud, empowered being living a life that's Instagram-worthy. And guess what? Every woman, especially the fierce ones around me, has her own stash of challenges, regrets, and heartbreaks.

I keep getting up because falling is just a pitstop, not a final destination. It's about standing up, learning from the faceplants, and, most importantly, being real. I play Sherlock with myself—am I being too hard, too selfish, or too fast-forward in my life?

Embrace the not-so-picture-perfect moments; they're like the sculptor's chisel molding you into a powerful, confident masterpiece. When despair knocks, remember the Hulk strength within you.

In an improv class, I learned that withholding thoughts is like being the party pooper. Participate with your unique, weird, fabulous perspective;

don't be stingy with your experiences. Listen to your heart; it's the oracle of your true desires.

Choices might be tough, but not making them is like bringing a spoon to a knife fight. True fulfillment came in my late 30s when I tapped into the source of me. I learned my likes and dislikes, gave myself a break, and tried different things. My heart swung open like a jazz club door because, honey, I stopped trying to fit into someone else's mold.

Resilience is your personal cruise ship through the stormy seas of life. Stand up, even if you fall like an awkward giraffe. Uncover your authentic self beneath the dusty carpet of people-pleasing.

To young women, the keys to the kingdom are right there in your sparkly bag. Soul-search, baby! Seek guidance but remember, the real wisdom lies in the quiet recesses of your fabulous mind and passionate heart. Comparison is so last season; embrace what makes you weirdly wonderful.

COVID didn't just bring masks and Zoom fatigue; it brought hours of joyful painting for me. Did I have the experience as an artist? No, I did not. In those strokes, the wild and weird warrior goddess in me emerged. A lightsaber and a paintbrush, who knew they made such a powerful combo? Turns out I opened an Etsy shop and sold those works of art which included jewelry! The beauty is that if I was stuck in comparison or self-doubt, I wouldn't have taken that risk.

So, darlings, who are you, and what will you create? The choice is as much yours as deciding between pizza and salad. Say "yes," "no," or the ambiguous "I don't know." Live out loud, like your life is a rock concert and you're the headliner. Because, my dears, that's where the real magic happens.

VIKKI ROOD

About Vikki Rood: Vikki Rood is a passionate advocate for joyful living, a seasoned empowerment coach, and a published author dedicated to helping individuals uncover their authentic selves and live lives filled with purpose, empowerment, and boundless joy. Vikki invites you to join her on a journey of self-discovery, empowerment, and joy.

Through coaching, workshops, and a thriving community, she'll help you uncover your authentic self, embrace your unique path, and find fulfillment in every facet of your life.

Author's Website: *www.VikkiRoodCoaching.com*

Book Series Website: *www.ThePrinciplesOfDebbieAndGoliath.com*

FEMALE EMPOWERMENT RESOURCES

In the journey of empowerment and overcoming challenges, it's crucial to have access to resources and support, especially in areas that profoundly affect women's lives. While The Principles of Debbie and Goliath book series is an inspiration and blueprint, we recognize the importance of direct support and advocacy. We highlight below some key resources:

Domestic Violence & Trafficking

- **Unsilenced Voices** [www.unsilencedvoices.org]: Unsilenced Voices (UV) is a global 501(c)3 nonprofit that empowers survivors of domestic violence, sexual assault, and human trafficking in multiple countries through advocacy, education, and support services.

- **National Domestic Violence Hotline** [www.thehotline.org]: This vital resource provides confidential support to victims of domestic violence and trafficking. They offer a 24/7 hotline, emergency services, and a wealth of information for those seeking help.

- **Rape, Abuse & Incest National Network** [www.rainn.org]: The nation's largest anti-sexual violence organization, RAINN operates the National Sexual Assault Hotline and carries out programs to prevent sexual violence, help survivors, and ensure that perpetrators are brought to justice.

- **The Slave Free Project** [www.slavefreeproject.com]: The Slave Free Project is building awareness and equipping others to prevent and fight human trafficking, breaking the silence and uniting communities to create the change the world has been waiting for.

- **Court Appointed Special Advocates** [www.nationalcasagal.org]: The National CASA/GAL Association for Children supports a network of 939 state CASA/GAL organizations and local CASA/GAL programs operating in 49 states (all but North Dakota) and the District of Columbia.

HABITS OF SUCCESS

Female Financial Literacy

- **National Endowment for Financial Education (NEFE)** [www.nefe.org]: NEFE is a nonprofit dedicated to improving financial literacy and effectiveness among all Americans. They provide a wealth of educational resources, research, and tools to empower women to make informed financial decisions.
- **Smart About Money** [www.smartaboutmoney.org]: A program of NEFE, this resource offers free courses and tools on a range of financial topics, from budgeting to saving for retirement, tailored to help women gain financial independence and literacy.
- **Women's Institute for Financial Education** [www.wife.org]: WIFE focuses specifically on empowering women with financial education. They offer seminars, workshops, and a variety of resources aimed at increasing financial knowledge and independence among women.
- **Napoleon Hill Foundation** [www.naphill.org]: The Napoleon Hill Foundation is a nonprofit educational institution dedicated to making the world a better place in which to live.

Military Family Support for Females

- **National Military Family Association** [www.militaryfamily.org]: This organization focuses on supporting military families through comprehensive programs such as spouse scholarships, child education initiatives, and wellness activities, with particular attention to the unique needs of female family members.
- **Blue Star Families** [www.bluestarfam.org]: Blue Star Families offers a range of support services, including career development, caregiving, and family support, specifically tailored to address the challenges faced by military spouses and female family members.
- **Service Women's Action Network** [www.servicewomen.org]: SWAN is dedicated to supporting, connecting, and advocating for servicewomen and female veterans. They offer resources, peer

support, and advocacy for issues including gender discrimination and military sexual trauma.

- **Center For Women Vets** [www.va.gov/womenvet/]: The Center for Women Veterans' (CWV) mission is to monitor and coordinate VA's administration of health care, benefits, services, and programs for women Veterans. We serve as an advocate for cultural transformation and to raise awareness of the responsibility to treat women Veterans with dignity and respect to #BringWomenVeteransHome2VA.

Additional Resources

- **World Youth Horizons** [www.worldyouthhorizons.com]: World Youth Horizons is a 501(c)(3)global non-profit organization that provides support to youth around the world by providing food, shelter, education, and experiences to help improve their economic conditions and to encourage youth to expand their horizons.

- **Unstoppable Foundation** [www.unstoppablefoundation.org]: The Unstoppable Foundation is a non-profit humanitarian organization bringing sustainable education to children and communities in developing countries thereby creating a safer and more just world for everyone. Their Mission: To ensure EVERY child has access to the life-long gift of an education.

- **Broadway Hearts** [www.broadwayhearts.org]: Broadway Hearts is a not-for-profit organization bringing professional Broadway performers, music, and joy to the extraordinary kids in treatment at children's hospitals nationwide.

- **God's Bucket Brigade** [www.godsbucketbrigade.org]: Blessing and loving the homeless and less fortunate with help for today, and hope for tomorrow.

- **Seek Her Foundation** [www.seekher.org]: SeekHer Foundation is on a mission to bridge the gender gap in mental health through advocacy, research, and support for emerging leaders who are impacting change in their local communities and beyond.

- **Lindsey Vonn Foundation** [www.lindseyvonnfoundation.org]: Impacting student-age girls 10-18 from underserved U.S.

communities with empowering self-esteem camps, and scholarships to participate in tech, sports and enrichment programs so that they can grow to be tomorrow's leaders and visionaries.

- **Girls Who Code** [www.girlswhocode.com]: Girls Who Code is a captivating after-school learning experience that introduces middle school and high school girls to computer science classes within a supportive sisterhood of peers. Thanks to rising women's tech events around the U.S. and woman-focused organizations, girls are becoming more and more exposed to careers in technology.

- **Girls Inc** [www.girlsinc.org]: In partnership with schools and at Girls Inc. centers, we focus on the development of the whole girl. She learns to value herself, take risks, and discover and develop her inherent strengths. The combination of long-lasting mentoring relationships, a pro-girl environment, and evidence-based programming equips girls to navigate gender, economic, and social barriers, and grow up healthy, educated, and independent.

- **Junior Habitude Warrior** [www.juniorhabitudewarrior.com]: Junior Habitude Warrior is an amazing organization providing strategies of growth for kids and teenagers focusing on building confidence, leadership, non-bullying, and personal development.

These organizations represent a beacon of hope and support for women facing these major issues. We encourage readers to utilize these resources and share them with those who might benefit from their services.

THE PRINCIPLES OF DEBBIE & GOLIATH

Habitude Warrior Mastermind

Join a team of
AWESOME
Entrepreneurs, Coaches, Business Owners, and Leaders to support you in your journey of success!

Be one of my personal guests for a session!
www.MastermindGuestPass.com

HABITUDE WARRIOR & INTEGRITY PUBLISHING EDITORIAL TEAM

Habitude Warrior International and Integrity Publishing take great pride in our editorial team who put their sweat, tears, and heart into each and every project and national bestseller! Thank you team!

JON KOVACH JR.
Team Manager

Jon Kovach Jr. strives to assist every author and every team member in the process of self-development for ultimate success.

PAT MINTON
VP of Operations

Pat Minton has been with the Habitude Warrior International team for over 20 years getting her start with Brian Tracy & Erik Swanson.

JILLIAN KOVACH
Editorial Manager

Jillian is a vital team member of Habitude Warrior & Integrity Publishing bringing her expertise managing our Editorial Department.

FATIMA HURD
Editorial Team & Photographer

Fatima is our Professional Photographer for Habitude Warrior as well as one of our members on the Proofing Department team.

LAUREN COBB
Editorial Team Member

Lauren Cobb is part of our Proofing Department for Habitude Warrior & Integrity Publishing as well as one of our authors.

To inquire about joining our team please send us an email to Team@HabitudeWarrior.com

THE PRINCIPLES OF DEBBIE & GOLIATH

HABITS OF SUCCESS

www.ingramcontent.com/pod-product-compliance
Ingram Content Group UK Ltd.
Pitfield, Milton Keynes, MK11 3LW, UK
UKHW020247240426
12048UKWH00027B/1645